CLAUDE MONTEFIORE AND CHRISTIANITY

Program in Judaic Studies
Brown University
BROWN JUDAIC STUDIES

Edited by
Jacob Neusner,
Wendell S. Dietrich, Ernest S. Frerichs, William Scott Green,
Calvin Goldscheider, David Hirsch, Alan Zuckerman

Project Editors (Project)

David Blumenthal, Emory University (Approaches to Medieval Judaism)
William Brinner (Studies in Judaism and Islam)
Ernest S. Frerichs, Brown University (Dissertations and Monographs)
Lenn Evan Goodman, University of Hawaii (Studies in Medieval Judaism)
William Scott Green, University of Rochester (Approaches to Ancient Judaism)
Norbert Samuelson, Temple University (Jewish Philosophy)
Jonathan Z. Smith, University of Chicago (Studia Philonica)

Number 157
CLAUDE MONTEFIORE AND CHRISTIANITY

by
Maurice Gerald Bowler

CLAUDE MONTEFIORE AND CHRISTIANITY

by
Maurice Gerald Bowler

Scholars Press
Atlanta, Georgia

CLAUDE MONTEFIORE AND CHRISTIANITY

© 1988
Brown University

Library of Congress Cataloging in Publication Data

Bowler, Maurice Gerald.
Claude Montefiore and Christianity.

(Brown Judaic studies ; no. 157)
Bibliography: p.
Includes index.
1. Montefiore, C. G. (Claude Goldsmid), 1858-1938.
2. Reform Judaism--Great Britain. 3. Montefiore, C. G.
(Claude Goldsmid), 1858-1938--Views on Christianity.
4. Christianity and other religions--Judaism.
5. Judaism--Relations--Christianity. I. Title.
II. Series.
BM755.M58B68   1989   296.8'346'0924   88-30830
ISBN 1-55540-286-0

Printed in the United States of America
on acid-free paper

Dedicated to the memory of

Levi Gertner & Meir Gertner

Contents

Preface

I would like to thank those who have helped in the writing of this book. Professor Raphael Loewe was a great help when this material was being prepared for the University College M. PHIL. and the staffs of various libraries have been very helpful. The busy people I have interviewed for background material have invariably been courteous and patient.

Special permission has been granted by the *Jewish Chronicle* of London for the inclusion of Chapter 6 "Montefiore's Three Mentors," most of which appeared in that journal on May 14th, 1982. Doctor Robert Gordis, editor of *Judaism*, has granted permission to publish chapter 1 "Claude Montefiore and his Quest," which appeared in the Fall 1981 issue. Also the quotations from Montefiore's letters to Solomon Schechter are included by "Courtesy of the Library of the Jewish Theological Seminary of America." These letters were edited by Dr. Joshua Stein in his book *Lieber Freund: The Letters of Claude Goldsmid Montefiore to Solomon Schechter, 1885-1902* and I am very grateful to him for allowing me to benefit from his work.

Naturally I accept responsibility for what appears in the book, but I am grateful to all who have helped me to learn while it was being written.

Maurice Bowler
London, 1987

Introduction

Claude Montefiore (1858-1938) was a well-educated and affluent English Jew who was inspired by the principles of 19th century cultural and religious Liberalism. This inspiration gave a breadth of vision which took in the whole of the then current Western European scene, as well as causing him to look far into the future. The dominant factor in this scene was not his own Jewish faith, nor Roman Catholicism. Rather, it was Protestant Christianity, and this because of the ascendancy of Great Britain and Germany, the Protestant leaders of Europe and the world. Because Montefiore was in touch with English and German theological writings, he was well aware that the apparently solid foundations of Protestant Christianity were subject to very considerable erosion due to the inroads of modern scholarship. This scholarship was revising considerably Protestantism's attitude to its touchstone, the Bible. Montefiore saw a similar "shaking of the foundations" in his own Jewish faith, and conceived the idea of a "new and purified Judaism" which would contain the best of both Jewish and Christian faiths and which would take over as a universal religion as the traditional forms of Christianity and Judaism withered away. In this scheme, Montefiore overlooked the residual momentum in both faiths which was to bring them both through their "turn of the century" crises. In order to facilitate his synthesizing work, Montefiore made himself master of the Christian sources in the New Testament, and also mastered contemporary radical scholarship pertaining to these sources. Much of his considerable literary output is taken up with Christian studies and the present thesis seeks to analyse Montefiore's treatment of Christian sources and themes. In order to understand more fully the influences which shaped his outlook, an examination of Montefiore's life and milieu precedes the analysis of his literary work.

Chapter One

Claude Montefiore & His Quest

... the relation of Liberal Judaism to the life and teaching of the historic Jesus, as well as to the books of the New Testament. This is one of the most important matters which has yet to be taken in hand.

C.G. Montefiore 1908[1]

His Background

Claude G. Montefiore (1858-1938), the founder of British Liberal Judaism, came from a very distinguished Anglo-Jewish family, the most famous member of which was Sir Moses Montefiore (1784-1885), the renowned Victorian philanthropist. If he had chosen to do so, Claude Montefiore could have become a respected leader in mainstream Anglo-Jewry, which in his day tended to look to its noble or upper class members for leadership. Montefiore's upper class credentials were impeccable as, after private tuition, he had gone to Balliol College, Oxford, where he had studied under Benjamin Jowett (1817-1893), and, after some rabbinic studies in Berlin had returned to a gentleman's life to follow his interest without having to follow a profession.

His Role

Montefiore's declared purpose was to ensure the survival of Judaism. In the *Jewish Religious Union & its Cause* he says "Our cause is, as we believe, the cause of Judaism."[2] Because he rejected the Zionist solution (of isolation *from* the Western world) and also the voluntary ghetto solution (of isolation *within* the Western world) he felt that Judaism had to be *reconstituted* if it was to meet the challenge of assimilation. By definition, the nature of the problem of assimilation and its solution must relate to the cultural force which was impinging on the Jewish community. In Montefiore's day this was a powerful Christianity, which in his youth influenced strongly the two main universities

---

[1]C.G. Montefiore, *Papers for Jewish People IV*, London, Jewish Religious Union, 1908, p.12.
[2]C.G. Montefiore, *The Jewish Religious Union & its Cause*, London, Jewish Religious Union, 1908, p.11.

in England, Oxford and Cambridge, which in turn influenced strongly the life of the nation. He said of the Jews of Britain and America "five/sixths of their conception of life are Christian."[3] This statement closely parallels that of Franz Rosenzweig (1886-1929) a later Jewish writer who faced a similar challenge in Germany, of which he said, "We are Christian in everything . . . our whole culture rests entirely on a Christian foundation."[4] Like Rosenzweig, Montefiore saw this as a challenge which could be met by absorbing the best of the surrounding culture and mobilizing what was absorbed in the service of Judaism. Rosenzweig said "In being Jews we must not give up anything, not renounce anything, but lead everything back to Judaism."[5] Montefiore similarly felt there was much in Christian culture, especially in the ethical teaching of Jesus, to enrich Judaism.[6] But whereas Rosenzweig opted for a "Two Covenant" system which "contained" Gentile Christians within a special Christian covenant with God, based on John 14:6 which would leave the Jewish people free to enjoy their own special covenant relationship with God,[7] Montefiore went beyond this "parallel lines" concept. Perhaps because he had never contemplated Christian baptism, as Rosenzweig had done, Montefiore was much more bold and daring in his treatment of Christianity and its leading characters and in this he is perhaps unique in this century. Because of the high standing which Montefiore gained as a scholar in Christian circles he was well placed to take a "Synoptic" view of both Judaism and Christianity. He well illustrates the saying "A genius sees what everybody else can see and thinks what nobody else has thought." It was obvious to all that the external Emancipation and the internal Enlightenment had loosened many of the traditional bonds which had held European Jewry together. Similarly Liberal Protestantism had loosened a great deal of Christian rigidity and much, even most of Christian doctrine in Liberal circles was in a state of flux, especially since modern Liberal scholarship had undermined the confidence of many Protestants regarding the Divine Inspiration and infallibility of the Bible, their main authority for doctrine. As Montefiore saw the need for Liberal Jews to understand Christianity, he applied himself to both Christian and Jewish sources, enlisting the aid of distinguished scholars and making himself master of the most advanced of Christian and Jewish scholarship. He wrote to his relative,

---

[3]C.G. Montefiore, *Papers for Jewish People XVI*, London, Jewish Religious Union, 1917, p.22.
[4]N. Glatzer, *Franz Rosenzweig – His Life & Thought*, New York, Schocken, 1961, p.19.
[5]F. Rosenzweig, 'On Jewish Learning,' *Contemporary Jewish Thought*, Washington, Ed. S. Noveck, Bnai Brith, 1969, p.223-224.
[6]C.G. Montefiore, *Papers for Jewish People XVI*, London, 1917, p.23, & *Liberal Judaism & Hellenism*, London, Macmillan 1918, p.86-87.
[7]N. Glatzer, *Franz Rosenzweig – His Life & Thought*, New York, Schocken, 1961, p.341.

Lucy Cohen, "I am the only English Jew living who can approach the gospels fairly impartially."[8] This claim, coming from an excessively modest man, has to be given considerable weight. As with Rosenzweig, his protracted studies in Christianity and apparent sympathy with Christian ideas were interpreted as a retreat from Judaism into something very like Christianity. This in spite of firm and clear rejection of the basic Christian doctrines by both men.

His Vision

Montefiore certainly did a great deal to interpret Judaism to Christians with lasting positive effect on Christian thought. His equally vigorous attempt to interpret Christianity to Jews was dogged with misunderstandings because it was so much out of line with Jewish thought. There was a long history of polemical writing on both the Christian and Jewish sides and a classic anti-Christian book, *Faith Strengthened*, by Isaac of Troki, was translated and distributed in the Jewish community only seven years before Montefiore's birth by Moses Mocatta. Both Jews and Christians were used to a disputational role in the past, although many of Montefiore's Christian readers, where they were not actually engaged in seeking to win over Jews to Christianity, seemed to be already tired of being adversaries. Christians were helped by Montefiore's books such as *The Religious Teaching of Jesus* (1910) and *Judaism & St. Paul* (1914) and Jews by such books as *Liberal Judaism* (1903) and *Outlines of Liberal Judaism* (1923) and many other books and pamphlets and articles. Montefiore's work was welcomed by Christians but the Jewish establishment and those for whom they spoke tended to view with suspicion any "irenic" treatment of Christianity.

The disciple of his later years, Rabbi Dr. Leslie Edgar, tells of Montefiore saying that "many Jewish friends had said to him 'You know Montefiore, I would join your movement if you would give up your preoccupation with Jesus and the Gospels.'" Rabbi Edgar continues, "I can still hear the ring of Montefiore's voice as he said: 'Of course I wouldn't.'"[9] But Montefiore was more than an interpreter. His vision of Judaism and Christianity led him to see both religions in a new light with remarkable possibilities for both.

His View of Christianity

Montefiore's views on Christianity were based on insights he had gained from such outstanding authorities as Benjamin Jowett (a Classicist with radical views on Scripture) at Oxford and in his later studies in the works of Harnack, Renan, Loisy and others in the forefront of Liberal Christian scholarship in his day. He also was helped by such Jewish scholars as Solomon Schechter, Israel

---

[8]Lucy Cohen, *Some Recollections of C.G. Montefiore*, London, Faber & Faber, 1940, p.77.
[9]L.I. Edgar, *Claude Montefiore's Thought & The Present Religious Situation*, London, Lib. Jewish Syn., 1966, p.21.

Abrahams and Herbert Loewe. Guided by Jowett's dictum that the student should "put himself *above* the documents"[10] (i.e., be scientifically detached), Montefiore would tend to see Christianity as the flexible, plastic entity which it had become in the hands of Liberal Christian scholars. In his eminently fair way he conceded that a religion is a whole, 'separable' only in the study of the scholar.[11] But this ideal view did not prevent him from carrying out this very separation in his treatment of Christianity, gladly acknowledging the sublimity of the statement of Jesus, "Nothing outside a man, entering into him, can make him unclean"[12] and disapproving strongly of the condemnation by Jesus of Pharisees and Rabbis.[13] The critical facility of being 'above the documents' left the scholar free to select what were felt to be authentic or acceptable statements of Jesus and withhold recognition from what were felt to be unworthy sentiments. The key to this treatment was the rejection of the doctrine of divine inspiration of scripture by Liberal Christian scholars. This was like switching off the current in a live electrical system, leaving the operator free to disconnect and remove components at will. Also by removing any suggestion of intrinsic divine authority from Jesus and the New Testament scriptures, they made it possible for non-Christian scholars such as Montefiore, who shared their basic pre-suppositions, to make use of the New Testament without incurring a charge of compromise. It was then possible to make the expression "divinely inspired" an editorial seal of approval rather than an *a priori* characteristic of holy writ as Paul affirms when he calls Scripture "Theopneustos" (2 Tim. 3:16). "The disciplined conscience and trained reason"[14] of the reader would recognise in selected writings an affinity with what he already knew of God's nature. On these premises, Montefiore as a Jew had more right of access to the Jewish writings of the New Testament than Gentile Liberal Christians who had reclassified the Christian scriptures as part of the general deposit of human literature. As we have seen, many of Montefiore's Jewish contemporaries did not share this freedom towards Christian things, preferring to define Christianity according to its own internally formulated definitions with their high view of Christ and the New Testament, both equally unacceptable to traditional Judaism. For them, the "current was still switched on" and the system was consequently dangerous and

---

[10]C.G. Montefiore, *Papers for Jewish People XV*, London, 1917, p.1, see also B. Jowett, *Dialogues of Plato*, Ed.3, vol.3, p.XXXVII, " . . . the consideration of their morality comes first, afterwards the truth of the documents in which they are recorded . . . we only learn the true lesson which is to be gathered from them when we place ourselves above them."

[11]C.G. Montefiore, *Papers for Jewish People XII*, London, Jewish Religious Union, 1916, p.5.

[12]C.G. Montefiore, *The Religious Teaching of Jesus*, London, Macmillan, 1919, p.48-49.

[13]ibid, p.53.

[14]C.G. Montefiore, *Papers for Jewish People X*, London, Jewish Religious Union, 1915, p.18.

to be avoided. Montefiore could say to his fellow Jews "Christianity was once the great *Antithesis* or antagonist . . . not so today"[15] and continuing the Hegelian process of Thesis versus Antithesis leading to Synthesis, he could go on to say that "merging" may come later.[16] His radical view of Christianity, combined with his equally radical view of Judaism, could take *him* on to such thoughts but he left most of his fellow Jews a long way behind him.

On Judaism

No dogmatic acceptance of the classic formulations of Judaism such as the Thirteen Principles of Maimonides (1135-1204) or its programmatic equivalent, the Shulḥan Arukh of Joseph Caro (1488-1575) or even the Torah, both written and oral, "given to Moses on Mount Sinai," inhibited Montefiore's development of thought. The critical axiom which seems to have transformed his attitude to Judaism and through him, the attitude of the whole British Liberal Jewish movement was that which stated that the Prophetic vision was prior to the Law, in time as well as in status.[17] Montefiore had good authority in contemporary biblical scholarship for this view, even if he was prepared to use this principle of priority in a more radical way than his friends and associates.[18] Herbert Loewe (1882-1940), his collaborator in *A Rabbinic Anthology* (1938), says "In one sense, Amos, Hosea and Isaiah precede the Law; in another sense the Law precedes them.If we are concerned with redaction, no doubt priority belongs to these prophets."[19] Loewe himself held this conviction about temporal precedence to be in full harmony with his position as an orthodox Jew, although many of his fellow orthodox Jews would have contested this. Montefiore, however, proceeding from the same premises, pushed on to the more radical Liberal position which made prophetic "Ethical Monotheism" the datum line of normative Judaism with "Mosaic" Law and Rabbinic Law taking honored but lower places in the development. This subordination of the letter to the spirit, giving the Law second place in time and significance, is reminiscent of St. Paul's description of the Law as something temporary, coming in after the promises to Abraham and being superseded by the New Covenant.[20] In Paul's case, the *promises to Abraham* outshine the Law but in both cases the principle of *subordination* of the Law is diametrically opposed to Maimonides, for instance, who says:

---

[15]C.G. Montefiore, *Papers for Jewish People XII*, London, Jewish Religious Union, 1916, p.8.
[16]ibid, p.15.
[17]C.G. Montefiore, *Papers for Jewish People IV*, London, Jewish Religious Union, 1908, p.7.
[18]C.G. Montefiore, *Papers for Jewish People VI*, London, 1910, p.12 etc.
[19]C.G. Montefiore & H. Loewe, *A Rabbinic Anthology*, New York, Greenwich/Meridan, 1938 (reprint undated) p.lxviii.
[20]Romans 4:13.

> I believe ... the prophecy of Moses ... was true, and that he was the chief of the prophets, both of those that preceded and of those that followed him. I believe ... the whole Law, now in our possession, is the same that was given to Moses ....[21]

In direct opposition to this, Montefiore states:

> We recognise no binding outside authority between us and God, whether in a man or in a book, whether in a church or in a code, whether in a tradition or in a ritual.[22]

He thus committed himself to a prophecy-oriented position in contrast to the Law-oriented position maintained by Jewish orthodoxy. Montefiore did not *reject* Law, just as his critics did not *reject* Prophecy, but the divergent attributions of priority, in every sense, polarized the Liberal and Orthodox positions. It would be misleading, of course, to class Montefiore with antinomian and iconoclastic critics of the Law and it would be unfair to see him as an advocate of mere "convenience" or "easy" Judaism. Montefiore could speak eloquently on the merits of the Law and its rabbinical exponents and the delight they took in fulfilling the Law and he was especially careful to make these emphases when expounding or defending Judaism before a Gentile audience or readership. Also, in spite of his abhorrence of nationalism and particularism in religion, he rejected the substitution of Sunday worship in place of Saturday worship, rejected intermarriage with non-Jews (other than proselytes), rejected the use of the New Testament in Jewish worship and insisted on the retention of circumcision – all in the interest of continuity and the avoiding of offence to the wider Jewish community.[23]

Conclusion

As we have seen above, significant segments within both Christianity and Judaism for a time, during Montefiore's earlier career, gave the impression of becoming more flexible towards each other in a world which itself seemed to be moving towards better things. The "irresistible force" of Christianity was much less so and the "immovable object" of Judaism seemed to be much less fixed than before (in both Liberal and Reform circles), but the passage of time seems to have shown these developments to be more cyclic than permanent. Because of this, Montefiore's self-chosen role as a catalyst between the two emerging progressive forces, Liberal Judaism and Liberal Christianity, was never fully realized, although he achieved a great deal.

---

[21] Authorised Daily Prayer Book, London, Eyre & Spottiswoode, 1957, Arts 7 & 8, p.90.
[22] C.G. Montefiore, *The Jewish Religious Union, its Principles & its Future* – private printing, 1909, cf Papers for Jewish People XXVII, 1927, p.21.
[23] ibid, p.18.

Inevitably, the challenge faced by Montefiore will have to be faced again and his response, however dated it may seem, will have to be brought out again for consideration, even though his conclusions may be as unacceptable now as they were in his day. Certainly there are few Jewish thinkers living today who can speak with greater authority, knowledge and insight into the relationship between Jews and their Christian neighbors than did Claude Montefiore in his own generation. Thanks largely to the interpretative address to Judaism that he himself did much to set in motion, Christian interpreters today are very much better equipped in regard to a knowledge of Judaism, its institutions, and theological implications than were those whom Montefiore addressed as his contemporaries.

Section One

EARLY CHRISTIAN INFLUENCES
& THEIR OUTWORKING

Chapter Two

Some Christian Models

[For] the Jews of Europe and of America ... who live in a Christian environment, and amid a civilisation which has been partially created by the New Testament, our right relation towards it must surely be of grave and peculiar importance. For this civilisation is also ours. The literature, which is soaked through and through with new Testament influences, is also *our* literature. The thought, which has been partially produced by the New Testament, is the thought amid which we are reared, which we absorb, to which we react. From every side, from every point of view, our attitude towards the New Testament is pressed upon us for consideration and settlement.... The very air we breathe, the moral, literary, artistic influences which we suck up from our childhood, are to a large extent, the same as those which surround and affect our Christian fellow-citizens.[1]

Introduction

Early in Montefiore's career, in 1893, a challenge was presented to him to elevate and improve his people the Jews by " ... devoting yourself to the Jewish race as the task of your life." This challenge was made by his old Balliol teacher, Benjamin Jowett, who sought to encourage him by saying, "Christianity has gone forward; ought not Judaism to make a similar progress ... ?"[2] This could perhaps be seen as a turning point in his life, a time when he would begin to look very closely at a developing Liberal Christianity as a model for an ideal Liberalized Judaism. In notes referred to by Prof. Cock of Southampton University,[3] Montefiore outlines his plans for a rejuvenated and purified Judaism, and the journal from which they are taken is dated 1883-86. So at this very early stage, when Montefiore was still quite

---

[1]C.G. Montefiore, *Liberal Judaism & Hellenism,* London, Macmillan, 1918, pp.78-79.
[2]Lucy Cohen, *Some Recollections of C.G. Montefiore,* London, Faber & Faber, 1940, p.59.
[3]ibid, pp.56-57, " ... he foresaw while scarcely out of his teens, the need of a reverent and sympathetic approach to biblical criticism, he held for a pruning of ritual and dogma, and he held for a fuller social clarity in Jewry, the need for a fuller social objective."

young (25-28),[4] we get a glimpse of the future leader of English Liberal Judaism probing into the future of his own religion, while under the influence of an outstanding thinker of another religion, Christianity. Although this thinker, Benjamin Jowett, (a specialist in Thucydides and Plato), the Master of Balliol College, Oxford, was his teacher in Classics, (known as "Greats"), he was also famous in the community at large (some would have said notorious) as the author of the chapter on "The Interpretation of Scripture" in the controversial *Essays and Reviews* published in 1860. From this essay Montefiore would have learned that the critical techniques used on classical writers could also be applied to the Holy Scriptures of Judaism and Christianity. This will need to be examined more closely in Chapter 5 under the heading of "The Question of Scriptural Inspiration," but from what has been said already it can be seen that there is some evidence that Montefiore's "technical" interest in Christianity, or at least some stimulus towards it, which led to his emergence as a recognised expert in Christian matters, could be dated from this period.

By Montefiore's own reckoning, however, as our opening quotation shows, the influence of a Christian milieu, such as would be experienced by a European or American Jew, was not something which could be said to begin at some stage in a person's formal education, when he felt sufficiently interested to investigate the religion of his neighbours. In Montefiore's view of the British and the American Jew, "five-sixths of their conception of life are Christian."[5]

The date on the Western Jew's morning newspaper would be generally understood to commemorate the incarnation of the Son of God. The first day of every week of his life would be visibly different from other days because it commemorated the resurrection of that same person. The names of places and building, hospitals and institutions would remind of St. Paul, St. Thomas and St. Bartholomew and even perhaps his own first name, and certainly the names of most of his Gentile friends and acquaintances would echo the names of Christian heroes. By a silent process of osmosis, the "Christian" nature of the surrounding culture would seep into his life and influence its character and even direction. Even if, as will be seen in Chapter 2, some of these influences were more cultural than strictly "Christian," they were none the less real. A deliberate attempt to locate and exclude these influences would be likely to rebound in a Freudian way, leading to what Montefiore called " . . . always thinking about Christianity," which he felt[6] was a trait of the orthodox Jewish community. If a sharp Jewish observer from a Moslem country such as Morocco had lived for a time with an "orthodox" Jewish family in Montefiore's England, he would have found evidence of "Christian" influence in the most neutral-seeming practices and expressions.

---

[4]ibid, p.56.

[5]C.G. Montefiore, *Papers for Jewish People XVI*, London, Jewish Religious Union, 1917, p.22.

[6]C.G. Montefiore, *Liberal Judaism & Hellenism*, London, Macmillan, 1918, pp.171-2.

What was so striking about Montefiore's approach to this problem was his frank recognition of the facts of the situation and his determination to preserve Jewish identity in spite of this or even to *mobilize* this problem so that it could become part of the solution to Anglo-Jewry's problems.

Montefiore's reflections on his own upbringing take on a special significance in the light of the above, especially as he says:

> ... my remarks about Jews are really to 90% of them simply childhood feelings and ways and ideas. Just as my religion is really only my childhood religion, and a little veneer! I don't think I have ever grown up or changed much![7]

His parents' provision for his religious education was complicated by the fact that his father was Lay Head of the Bevis Marks Spanish & Portuguese Synagogue, whereas his mother was an enthusiastic member of the West London Reform Synagogue, which was largely the result of a breakaway from Bevis Marks. A very revealing and significant light is thrown on the philosophy of the West London Synagogue (where Montefiore was brought up) by his son, Leonard Montefiore, who says:

> In 1842 ... it was of the utmost importance to make the Synagogue service resemble, in externals at all events, the service of the Church.[8]

Montefiore himself, however, having been born in the year when full civil equality was granted to British Jews (1858), and going up to Oxford after religious tests for entry had already been abolished (1871) would perhaps see the understandable pragmatism of his synagogue as rather outdated. He also recalls the minister, Rev. Mr. Marks (his tutor in Judaism), and his uncritical attitude to scripture,[9] and this minister's categorizing of the Greeks as those who taught the world about Beauty,[10] seemed to him later as a rather simplistic and naive approach to Hellenism, which at University came to mean so much to him, and continued to shape his thinking throughout his life. A vital factor in Jewish life – the close interaction of a tightly-knit community, seems to have been missing from his life. Of the many visitors to the Montefiore home, few, apart from relatives, were Jewish. In addition to religious instruction from Rev. Mr. Marks, Mr. (later Sir) Philip Magnus tutored Montefiore in general subjects but the vital preparation for University entrance was entrusted to two Christian

---

[7]Lucy Cohen, *Some Recollections of C.G. Montefiore*, London, Faber & Faber, 1949, p.135.

[8]Stein & Aaronsfeld, L.G. Montefiore, In Memoriam, London, Vallentine & Mitchell, 1964, p.12, ("Here (W. London Synagogue) Mr. Marks taught the verbal inspiration of the Pentateuch" p.71.)

[9]C.G. Montefiore, *Liberal Judaism & Hellenism*, London, Macmillan, 1918, p.2 cf pp.71-2.

[10]ibid, pp.184-5.

clergymen, the first of whom was Mr. (later Dean) Arthur Page.[11] Montefiore's parents had considered his health too delicate for an education at school[12] but their decision to provide only home tuition deprived him of an education among those of his own age with all the natural stimulus and opportunity to interact with others that this would bring. Their decision to bring in as tutors cultured representatives of the majority faith would certainly help Montefiore to understand the surrounding culture, and the undivided attention of educated adult minds would have a stimulating effect, perhaps to the exclusion of a more slow and natural process of development amongst peers, but the significant factor is that the influence which had most access to his mind at this vital stage of his development was steeped in Christianity. This is not to say that his tutor, Mr. Page, would be in any way disposed to convert or proselytize his young charge, in fact it can be taken for granted that he would do his utmost to inculcate in him a respect and reverence for the Jewish heritage. But young people, especially a highly intelligent youth such as Montefiore undoubtedly was, tend to ask questions and faced with an opportunity that most young Jews did not have, he would naturally satisfy his curiosity about the established religion of the country. So from his tutors' expert knowledge of Christianity, he would be able to extract a more than usual knowledge of Christianity for himself, no matter how guarded his tutors' replies might be. Lucy Cohen records that Montefiore could worship together with Mr. Page in church or synagogue.[13] Making the natural assumption that this refers to the period of Mr. Page's tutorship, an obvious question arises. What would be the effect of immersing a young Jew in an atmosphere of inspiring Christian music, antiquated but inspiring language in surroundings of quiet beauty, in the company of a respected adult who would himself value the experience very highly? Certainly it would at the very least influence him towards the decorum of his later Liberal Judaism. If he had been able to contrast this atmosphere with that of the rather uninhibited orthodox Jewish "shtibl" it would have been different. As it was, his own synagogue, the West London Reform synagogue at Upper Berkeley St., London, was, as we have seen above, organized to " . . . resemble in externals at all events, the service of the Church.[14] So in the Anglican service he was experiencing the original, of which his own particular synagogue service was but a copy. Mr. Page's place as tutor was taken by Mr. (later Rev.) Glazebrook, who became a church dignitary at Ely.[15]

---

[11]Lucy Cohen, *Some Recollections of C.G. Montefiore*, London, Faber & Faber, 1940, p.37.
[12]ibid, p.37.
[13]ibid, p.39.
[14]Stein & Aaronsfeld, *L.G. Montefiore, In Memoriam*, London, Vallentine & Mitchell, 1974, p.24.
[15]Lucy Cohen, *Some Recollections of C.G. Montefiore*, London, Faber & Faber, 1940, p.38.

Apart, however, from Christian doctrines which may or may not have interested him at the time, it would be inevitable that Montefiore would imbibe Christian values (i.e. ethical and other standards derived from New Testament teaching). Without going into the issue of whether or not these would be better or worse than Jewish values, the least that could be said is that they would be *different*. Therefore, on the principle of "what you *are* speaks louder than what you *say*," he would have been deeply impressed with the standards expected of a Victorian Christian gentleman, which his tutors would inevitable exemplify in their day-to-day behaviour. These would include a certain cold dignity in controversy, a self-denying concern for others' wishes and a deference to the opinions of others, "turning the other cheek," loving one's enemies, the ideal of "saintliness," of ascetic benevolence which Victorians looked for in the biographies of their heroes and heroines and which, sometimes in defiance of the facts, they usually found. Some of these qualities are paralleled in Stoicism and in the Roman concept of "gravitas," and were valued by non-Christian Victorians, but in general they were associated with the Christian ideal. In his later New Testament studies, Montefiore was to even criticize Jesus for what he felt was a lack of these "Christian" virtues because Jesus was so outspoken in his condemnation of the scribes and Pharisees![16] This of course raises the issue of the definition of the term "Christian" which is defined in Acts 11:26 as a *disciple* of Christ but which has been used in a variety of other ways. In any case, it does seem that Montefiore would have come to his New Testament studies with a *culturally* formed picture of what a Christian should be. But most important for the present purpose of ascertaining early Christian influences on him, it does seem that the norms which Montefiore set for his life were to a considerable extent influenced by non-Jewish and especially Christian values. Even the classical studies which were obligatory as he prepared for University, and which claimed his main attention in his LIT. HUM. syllabus at Balliol College, were mediated through Anglican channels such as Jowett and others. Although Christian presuppositions might not obtrude into the instruction, they could hardly have been entirely without influence.

Because of the importance given in English higher education to what Matthew Arnold once called the "grand, old, fortifying classical curriculum"[17] we must accept Montefiore's many quotations and allusions to the classics as evidence of their influence on him. Benjamin Jowett had written to him in January 1893, "The Jews . . . ought not to fall short of the highest, whether gathered from the teaching of Jesus or from Greek philosophy."[18] Because of the special role that classical sources played in 19th century Christian thought, any

---

[16]C.G. Montefiore, *Liberal Judaism & Hellenism*, London, Macmillan, 1918, p.108.
[17]*Christianity Today*, Oct. 10th, 1980, Dover, N.J. quoted by J.D. Douglas
[18]Lucy Cohen, *Some Recollections of C.G. Montefiore*, London, Faber & Faber, 1940, p.59.

comprehensive interpretation of the "Christianity" which influenced Montefiore and his fellow Jews in Europe must include this "assimilated" Hellenism as part of the overall picture. Disraeli, a very acute observer of the English scene which he was later to dominate, draws attention to the "pagan" element in "Christian" education in a satirical exchange between two of the characters in his novel *Tancred*. Queen Astarte of the Ansaray, herself a 19th century worshipper of the Greek gods, says of her visitor, Tancred, Lord Montacute, " . . . the reason he was acquainted with the god-like forms is, that in his country it is the custom (custom to me most singular, and indeed incomprehensible) to educate the youth by teaching them the ancient poems of the Greeks, poems quite lost to us, but in which are embalmed the sacred legends." Her companion Fakredeen replies, "We ought never to be surprised at anything that is done by the English . . . who are, after all, in a certain sense, savages . . . their religion is an exotic; and as they are indebted for that to Syria, it is not surprising that they should import their education from Greece."[19] Disraeli was brought up as an Anglican but, like Montefiore, was descended from Italian Jews. Looking at the same phenomenon, however, Montefiore saw nothing amusing or incongruous about importing education from Greece and claimed " . . . there is kinship between Hellas and Judea, therefore we can fuse the spirit of Hellas with our own. And this kinship with Greece Liberal Jews will feel the more acutely, because, like the Greeks . . . we were a petty nation; we became a spirit."[20] This is a Judaism which has travelled far from the days of the Maccabees, but the Christians amongst whom Montefiore learned of the "spirit of Hellas" had also travelled far from the days of Tertullian (c. 160-240) who said, "Away with all projects for a 'Stoic,' a 'Platonic' or a 'dialectic' Christianity!"[21] Montefiore makes the point that "It is a commonplace that Christianity conquered the world partly because it underwent a considerable infiltration from Hellenism."[22] This is a statement worth examining, but when Paul's epistles are compared with the great Christian masterpiece by John Milton, *Paradise Lost*, it is in the English Puritan we read of "Hermione and Cadmus, Ammonian Jove and Olympias," not in the student of Gamaliel. This post-Renaissance Classicism helped to form the scholars who in their turn gave to Montefiore his earliest and perhaps strongest impressions of "Christianity." When therefore his "indebtedness" to Christianity is assessed, even where Montefiore makes an open acknowledgement of borrowing from Christian thought, it is as well that the source in question should be examined to see how much of it is basic, credal, New Testament Christianity and how much is of a developed or augmented or even incongruous

---

[19]B. Disraeli, *Tancred*, London, Longmans Green & Col, 1919, pp.436-437.
[20]C.G. Montefiore, *Liberal Judaism & Hellenism*, London, Macmillan, 1918, p.230.
[21]*Documents of the Christian Church*, OUP, London, 1965, p.8.
[22]C.G. Montefiore, *Liberal Judaism & Hellenism*, London, Macmillan, 1918, p.188.

nature. There are certain interesting features of Montefiore's life and work and teaching, which have strong affinities with the Christianity of his day, but which will repay a more than superficial examination.

The Gentleman

The Oxford Dictionary defines the term "gentleman" with such phrases as "man of good social position or of wealth and leisure" or "of no occupation" but its associations of identity and belonging and social acceptance were the characteristics of his own class which Montefiore longed to see shared by his fellow Jews in England.[23] Emancipation had come in 1858, and Oxford and Cambridge became accessible to Jews in 1871, but Jowett, in his letter of January 1893 referred to above, urged Montefiore to set about "endeavouring to raise the manners and ways of their teachers and educators."[24] What neither Jowett nor Montefiore would have paid much attention to was the fact that in England, the term "gentleman" tended to mean in the 19th century "Christian gentleman," even if the doctrinal or even some moral elements of Christianity were not insisted on. Nevertheless, Dr. Arnold of Rugby's ideal of the Christian gentleman was very familiar to all graduates of public schools, and even those who studied under private tutors at home, like Montefiore, would be well aware of what was expected of a gentleman. Montefiore uses the terms of the day such as "good form"[25] in his writings and his continual self-depreciation in terms such as "I am an average man myself"[26] expressed the kind of modesty expected of a gentleman. Also a gentleman had to keep calm and if possible be "gentle" and this famous "sangfroid" is referred to by A.L. Rowse in his account of 19th century Oxford. He quotes Santayana as saying " . . . the Englishman . . . carries his English weather in his heart wherever he goes, and it becomes a cool spot in the desert, and a steady and sane oracle amongst all the deliriums of mankind."[27] So when we hear Montefiore saying " . . . self-control, temperance, the cultivation of the mind, inward refinement and good taste, these are the ideas and ideals that we have won from Hellas,"[28] it may be pertinent to ask how much the English, Christian channel has shaped the Hellenic ideal that Montefiore had embraced and wanted to commend to his fellow Jews. The self-

---

[23] Stein & Aaronsfeld, *L.G. Montefiore, In Memoriam,* London, Vallentine & Mitchell, 1964, p.67.

[24] Lucy Cohen, *Some Recollections of C.G. Montefiore,* London, Faber & Faber, 1940, p.59.

[25] C.G. Montefiore, *Papers for Jewish People VII,* London, Jewish Religious Union, 1913, p.9.

[26] ibid, p.12.

[27] A.L. Rowse, *Oxford in the History of England,* New York, G. Putnam's & Sons, 1975, p.235.

[28] C.G. Montefiore, *Liberal Judaism & Hellenism,* London, Macmillan, 1918, p.223.

depreciation he so much admired and practised could be attributed to his heeding the classical warning against "Insolent excess, Hubris"[29] or it could be traced to the influence of Paul's statement in 1 Corinthians 13 "charity vaunteth not itself, is not puffed up," which was a favourite New Testament passage of Montefiore's[30] or it might just be "good form." Dean Inge, an influential thinker in Montefiore's day, quotes a writer in the *Hibbert Journal for April 1905* as saying that the code of honour and chivalry is the real religion of most laymen. The Dean goes on to comment "The idea of a gentleman is the fine flower of our national character . . . it is the finest ideal which a nation has ever set before itself. To it we owe most of the things in our history of which we may reasonably be proud." He also comments "That a great many English gentlemen are sincere Christians goes without saying and it is often assumed . . . that the two words are almost interchangeable. This is the staple moral teaching in our public schools. Nor do I see anything amiss in this amalgamation of the two ideals."[31] But the net result of this 19th century amalgam of Stoicism and Christianity was sometimes a rather inhibiting self-abnegation. Montefiore was a diligent and competent scholar, a highly moral but also kind, compassionate and generous man, but in conformity with custom, felt obliged to minimize his scholarship and moral stature.

Hillel's dictum, "If I am not for myself, who will be for me? And being for myself, what am I? And if not now, when?"[32] (as it is usually translated) would have supplied a corrective here, not to stifle modesty, nor to promote arrogance, but to introduce an element of balance and *amour propre*. Also the gentlemanly dislike of argument and controversy has its drawbacks as well as its advantages. Dr. W.R. Matthews, Dean of St. Paul's, could say of his friend Montefiore "He had a wonderful tolerance and readiness to appreciate points of view not his own."[33] Bishop Gore could say of Montefiore that the best Christian he knew was a Jew.[34] But Montefiore himself seems to have thought that sometimes the more rugged qualities of character are needed to make one's mark in this world. This is expressed in his address "Old and New" where he says "The philosopher in his chamber may attempt to be fair all round, to satisfy every need and claim, but if he seek to carry his fairness into action, it will probably result in sterility. In human affairs to be completely balanced seems to end in sheer suspense . . . in religion . . . the persons who have set their mark upon

---

[29] ibid, p.199.

[30] ibid, pp.116-117.

[31] W.R. Inge, *Christian Ethics & Modern Problems*, London, H. & Stoughton, 1930, pp.337-338.

[32] *Pirke Avot*, 1:14.

[33] W.R. Matthews, *C.G. Montefiore, the Man and his Thought*, University of Southampton, 1956, p.23.

[34] Ch. Bermant, *The Cousinhood*, London, Eyre & Spottiswoode, 1971, p.322.

action have usually been somewhat one-sided."[35] Was he speaking from his experience as a would-be reformer and radical? Norman Bentwich said of him "He has a wonderful talent of stating the case he opposed fairly and almost convincingly."[36]

Noblesse Oblige

The ordinary motives for the decent and honourable life . . . good form, the pressure of environment; the voice of conscience; the service of the state; *noblesse oblige;* the ugliness of vice; the beauty of virtue; the desire to please one's parents and several others!"[37]

Another concept which had a considerable influence in Montefiore's day was the notion that rank and privilege carried with them obligation. This principle can be found in the New Testament axiom "For unto whomsoever much is given, of him shall be much required" (Luke 12:48). This might be seen as being parallel with the social convention of "noblesse oblige" listed above by Montefiore, if St. Paul had not reminded us that "Not many mighty, not many noble are called" (I Corinthians 1:26). The New Testament does not seem to envisage the Church as an established and privileged body, supported by the noble and rich, and Montefiore himself suggests in his essay on Liberal Judaism and Democracy[38] that religion has been used too often in the past to actually support the noble and the rich themselves. But there can be exceptions such as The Countess of Huntingdon giving great support to the early Methodists and William Wilberforce leading the fight against slavery abroad, and Lord Shaftesbury leading the fight against industrial slavery in England. Throughout the 19th century there was a great surge of service by the privileged on behalf of the needy, as Dr. Kathleen Heasman has shown in her thesis, "Evangelicals in Action – an appraisal of their social work in the Victorian era."[39] The kind of worker who is dismissed by many today as a "do-gooder" and the kind of work which is now often done by trained and well-paid "social workers," was the province of unpaid volunteers or modestly paid professionals who were sponsored by well-to-do people with a social conscience. Public benefactors built churches, hospitals and schools, and it was perhaps the impact of these "Christian good workers," more than the theological justification for them, which helped to stimulate Montefiore and kindred spirits to similar efforts. To use St. Paul's phrase, they were "provoked to emulation" (Romans 11:14)

[35]C.G. Montefiore, *Jewish Addresses,* London, Brimley Johnson, 1904, p.151.
[36]Norman Bentwich, *Claude Montefiore & his Tutor in Rabbinics,* University of Southampton, 1966, p.14.
[37]C.G. Montefiore, *Papers for Jewish People VII,* London, Jewish Religious Union, 1913, p.9.
[38]C.G. Montefiore, *Liberal Judaism & Hellenism,* London, Macmillan, 1918, p.260.
[39]K. Heasman, *Evangelicals in Action,* London, Geof. Bles, 1962.

although not in the exact sense that the apostle meant. Of his own activities, Montefiore said "I feel it incumbent, as a Jew, to do just a little more than is absolutely necessary."[40] This was certainly a masterpiece of understatement because Montefiore's benefactions were many, widespread, very generous and often anonymous. His help was given not merely from his money, of which he had a great deal, but also from his time.

In the field of Education he helped the Froebel Institute in its training of teachers, and in addition to giving considerable financial help he was its honorary secretary from 1882 when only 23 years of age. It was in his capacity as staff interviewer that he met his first wife, Theresa Schorstein, who had come to apply for a post at the Institute.[41] They were married in 1886, and when she died tragically in 1889, leaving a son, Leonard, Montefiore turned to the Institute to help him in the education of his motherless child. Leonard, in his turn, continued the 'Montefiore tradition' in watching over the welfare of the institute, and it was said of their combined influence that it was characterized by a " . . . respect for human personality in a free society; respect for liberal scholarship and learning; and a faith in the supreme importance of spiritual values."[42] At the other end of the educational spectrum, Montefiore was vice-president of the Hartley College, later to become the University of Southampton, in 1908 and from 1913-1934 President, serving from 1927 as Chairman of the General Purposes Committee. This willingness to actually *work* for good causes as well as to act as a "patron" was a remarkable feature of Montefiore's service for his fellow men, both Jew and Gentile.[43]

Another remarkable quality possessed by Montefiore was his ability to inspire others to take up the same kind of unselfish service that he was performing. In addition to the instance of his own son's following his example as Chairman of the Froebel Educational Institute (a position now filled by his grandson, Alan), as touched on above, he also in 1911-12 encouraged his son and his son's friend Basil Henriques (already prompted to youth service by Alec Patterson) to work at Canon Barnett's social work settlement "Toynbee Hall," and was a great help to Henriques in the founding and support of his Oxford & St. Georges settlement in the East End of London and also in the work of Lily Montagu, and her girls' club work especially.

Once again, the existence of working models of Christian settlements and youth clubs as an example and incentive to Jewish emulation can be seen as a decisive factor in the initiatives which Montefiore and his associates took. An

---

[40]Lucy Cohen, *Some Recollections of C.G. Montefiore*, London, Faber & Faber, 1940, p.252.
[41]ibid, p.50.
[42]Stein & Aaronsfeld, *L.G. Montefiore, In Memoriam*, London, 1964, p.108.
[43]W.R. Matthews, *C.G. Montefiore, the Man and his Thought*, University of Southampton, 1956, p.3.

interesting early note about this is found in the Jewish Addresses given in the 1902-3 services of Montefiore's Jewish Religious Union in which Rev. A. Wolf says in his address of March 28th 1903 that a " . . . Jewish adaptation of the now familiar University settlement seems to have everything in its favour," involving the "co-operation of University men, and the better educated generally."[44]

The Good Samaritan

Leading on from Montefiore's general philanthropic activity, we come to an enterprise which was very closely tied in with a Christian emphasis which he never tired of commending to his fellow Jews. In his essay 'Liberal Judaism and the New Testament,' after mentioning the New Testament parables of the Good Samaritan and the Prodigal Son,[45] he says "That God loves the repentant sinner is a familiar Old Testament doctrine, that man should *search out* and *cause* the sinner to repent by the compulsion of love, adds a new touch, a new truth, a new moral ideal. 'Rejoice with me, for I have found my sheep which was lost.'"[46] Later he adds " . . . the hall marks of the Gospel teaching are displayed in the bidding, not merely to help the poor and the suffering when they come your way, but to seek them out, and not merely to help the good, but also the outcast, the pariah and the sinner. Hence it is that all regenerative and redemptive labour and devotion among the Gentile world look back, and look up, to the words and the practice of Jesus as to their source and their stimulus. And justly . . . . And now . . . comes the demand not to leave the sinner alone to repent if he chooses but to *cause* him to repent, to work regeneration and the new heart within him by deeds of sympathy or words of love."[47]

The principle of the compassionate rescue of the fallen, which Montefiore expresses so beautifully in these words, is expressed just as beautifully in his actual work for Jewish women and girls, but the interesting thing is that the practical work began in 1885 at the instigation of his relative Lady Battersea, whereas the words were not written till around 1914 and published in 1918. What was perhaps Montefiore's most outstanding and characteristic work of philanthropy was started because his relatives, Lady Battersea and her sister, had been approached by a Christian social worker who had encountered two Jewish women among the prostitutes among whom she was working at the London Docks. Lady Battersea, who described Montefiore was "my dear and valued cousin . . . the most generous of individuals, with the purest and noblest of minds," asked him to go, with Rev. S.L. Singer, to the Docks to see if anything

[44]C.G. Montefiore, *Jewish Addresses,* London, Brimley Johnson, 1904, p.133.
[45]C.G. Montefiore, *Liberal Judaism & Hellenism,* London, Macmillan, 1918, p.86.
[46]ibid, p.87.
[47]ibid, p.107.

could be done to rescue these women, but they were unsuccessful. Montefiore, probably realizing that he could be of more help in organizing and supporting the efforts of others in this kind of work, gave this support to the efforts of Lady Battersea, the Hon. Mrs. Yorke and Lady Rothschild in their forming of the "Jewish Association for the Protection of Women and Girls" to carry out this work.[48] He joined their "Gentlemen's Committee" and in 1906 became chairman of the International and Parliamentary Committee, becoming vice-president in 1913 and chairman of the International Bureau in 1929. Montefiore did not again become involved in interviewing the women being helped, but did a great deal, including attending conferences in different parts of Europe, to help to crush the white slave traffic which was holding so many helpless women in bondage. Lucy Cohen records that Montefiore "abhorred men who live by exploiting defenceless women" and he asked for "compassion and sympathy with their victims."[49] This certainly links up with the attitude of Jesus to the condemned adulteress in St. Luke 7:47[50] as Montefiore says of Jesus "We note . . . a certain gentleness in Jesus . . . even towards an adulteress . . . he perceived that the cause of woman's fall is too often the vileness and cruelty of man."[51] This comment also was published in 1918 and written not long before. Montefiore was well aware of the need to protect the reputation of the Jewish community in this matter and was especially concerned to eliminate the regrettable Jewish involvement in this traffic, as Lucy Cohen records,[52] so his work was of great benefit for Anglo-Jewry in general as well as for its casualties.

The Saint

What impressed everyone who knew him was – I think there is no other word for it – his saintliness.

Rt. Hon. H.A.L. Fisher[53]

Dean Matthews was a close personal friend of Claude Montefiore and it is significant that he says of him that he brought to his studies "the temper, the presuppositions, and the method of nineteenth century liberal culture."[54] This is

---

[48]Lucy Cohen, *Some Recollections of C.G. Montefiore*, London, Faber & Faber, 1940, pp.147-151.
[49]ibid, p.151.
[50]C.G. Montefiore, *Liberal Judaism & Hellenism*, London, Macmillan, 1918, p.110, cf p.107.
[51]ibid, p.110.
[52]Lucy Cohen, *Some Recollections of C.G. Montefiore*, London, Faber & Faber, 1940, p.147.
[53]W.R. Matthews, *C.G. Montefiore, the Man and his Thought*, University of Southampton, 1956, p.6.
[54]ibid, p.11. See *Some Recollections of C.G. Montefiore, p.227* "A good Victorian."

a very significant observation because although Montefiore was only in his early forties when the Victorian era ended with the old Queen's death in 1901, Montefiore was one of those who had been formed by the Victorian era and he took with him into the new century many of the values and attitudes of the former era. The ideal of the "English gentleman" has been already mentioned but it is apposite here to quote Dean Inge's statement that critics of the "gentleman" ideal " . . . may even argue that since his virtues are partly based on self respect, which they miscall pride, they are only 'splendid vices.'"[55] This challenge leads us on to a higher plane in the Victorian categories of character and although the concept of the saint might seem at first distinctly religious and specifically Christian, this judgement meets a check when we read of Gilbert Murray (1866-1957), "the foremost Hellenist of his time" that he was "a secular saint." Secular in that he was "a complete rationalist, without any religious sense" and a *saint* in that "He was an astonishingly rounded human being, with brilliant gifts of mind, essentially happy and well adjusted."[56] Victorian England was not completely free from examples of neurotic and masochistic approaches to saintliness, but at least in the Liberal Protestant circles in which Montefiore encountered Christianity, he would come across the ideal of "charity . . . humility . . . unselfishness . . . sweetness of temper" and "transparent honesty and integrity," all of which terms are used by a Gentile contemporary to describe Montefiore.[57] The pictorial representation of this ideal can be seen in Holman Hunt's picture "The Light of the World" and in countless stained glass windows and religious book illustrations, in children's books especially. The world is a better place for such people and all who have been touched by the lives of such individuals can testify of the reassuring and healing influence which emanates from them. But although such "saints" are an adornment to any religion it was rather confusing of Bishop Gore to say of Montefiore that "the best Christian he knew was a Jew"[58] even if his comment was whimsical. As Montefiore's son Leonard remarked of another Jew about whom this was said, " . . . Christians are apt to call [these] the Christian virtues, but [they] could equally well be described as Jewish virtues."[59]

Montefiore was obviously taken up with the "saintly" ideal (in its more healthy form) because he asked in an introductory address to the Jewish

---

[55]W.R. Inge, *Christian Ethics & Modern Problems*, London, H & Stoughton, 1930, p.339.

[56]A.L. Rowse, *Oxford in the History of England*, New York, G. Putnam's & Sons, 1975, p.225.

[57]W.R. Matthews, *C.G. Montefiore, the Man and his Thought*, University of Southampton, 1956, p.6.

[58]Ch. Bermant, *The Cousinhood*, London, Eyre & Spottiswoode, 1971, p.322.

[59]Stein & Aaronsfeld, *L.G. Montefiore, In Memoriam*, London, Vallentine & Mitchell, 1964, p.83.

Religious Union in 1902[60] "are we materialists, lacking in *saintliness* and religious ardour?" Also in the unlikely context of his essay on 'Liberal Judaism and Democracy' he says "The saints form an aristocracy, whether democracy like it or no . . . . Our reverence for God, our humility before Him, enable us the better to feel reverence and humility towards those who, among men, are wiser, better, holier than ourselves."[61] Also in a sermon preached in America he said " . . . religion . . . requires not only its righteous heroes, but its spiritual saints. I think the Jews run some risk of forgetting this."[62] Also in his pamphlet 'What would you have us do?' he answers those Jews who ask him this question by challenging them to "Become saints."[63] Montefiore's more traditional fellow-Jews would have perhaps found the call to scholarship more congruous. His call for "general" saintliness would also tend to clash with the ancient Jewish concept of an elite of thirty-six hidden saints on whose qualities the world was thought to depend.

But the very fact of declaring that his programme included the promotion of saintliness and the producing of Liberal Jewish saints who would show the kind of qualities which others saw in him (although Montefiore never openly made this application, nor would ever have claimed himself to be a saint), raised problems. It implied a present dearth of saintliness in Judaism, and this seems to have stirred up Solomon Schechter, Montefiore's old mentor, to refute this charge. In his essay "Saints & Saintliness," Schechter is at pains to show that Judaism, just like other religions, has its saints. As his essay seems from the preface to its 1908 publication to have been written after Montefiore's challenge about "saintliness," the 1902 address would have been available to Schechter. Indeed, a reference to "elasticity" in Schechter's essay[64] looks so much like an allusion to the very next address in Montefiore's series[65] that it rather looks as if Schechter could have had Montefiore's book before him as a "vorschrift" as he wrote his essay. Schechter makes a succession of points which are specific contradictions of Montefiore's view on dietary laws, festivals, eclecticism, etc., and he gives examples of Jewish saints who show the required qualities of meekness, humility and self-control generosity and chastity. But part way through he seems to explode his own argument by saying, "Of course, there were other saints who were distinguished more by their zeal than by their powers of persuasion. They were *good haters* and Elijah was their model but it may be

---

[60]C.G. Montefiore, *Jewish Addresses,* London, Brimley Johnson, 1904, p.14.
[61]C.G. Montefiore, *Liberal Judaism & Hellenism,* London, Macmillan, 1918, p.260.
[62]Free Synagogue Pulpit, vol. 11:6-7, June-July, 1910, New York.
[63]C.G. Montefiore, *Papers for Jewish People VII,* London, Jewish Religious Union, 1913, p.13, cf *A Rabbinic Anthology, p.232.*
[64]S. Schechter, *Studies in Judaism,* vol. 2, Philadelphia, Jewish Publication Society, 1908, p.148.
[65]C.G. Montefiore, *Jewish Addresses,* London, Brimley Johnson, 1904, p.68.

said in their favour, that as far as Judaism is concerned their motives were pure; their zeal was never dictated by consideration of self or by ambition. Sometimes I am inclined to think that the haters and the lovers were both right."[66] This last sentence suddenly polarizes Schechter's and Montefiore's views of sainthood so that they are revealed in stark antithesis. There was very little room for hatred or violence or anger in the Victorian stereotype of the saint and it could be that Montefiore and others like him who aspired to sainthood of this type or at least held it before themselves as an ideal as he quite clearly did, were taking on themselves a crippling burden. Montefiore talks quite often about "The defects of virtues" in which he refers to the familiar Aristotelian concept of qualities being found in associated pairs so that every virtue tends to carry with it the danger of an associated defect. Examples of this would be Zeal and Impatience, Serenity and Apathy, Generosity and Improvidence, etc. The "shadow" associated with Victorian saintliness was an *impotence* in the dynamics of everyday relationships. Sir Samuel Gurney-Dixon, in describing Montefiore's character in his introduction to Dean Matthew's 1st Montefiore Memorial Lecture, certainly has this problem in mind when he says, "In spite of the gentleness which characterized him he was not weak, but could be firm and resolute, and on occasion display anger . . . but this was rare in him . . . ."[67] But impotence in certain situations may be due not to weakness of character but to acquired inhibitions; the "saintly" persona which Montefiore may have been born to, or which he may have acquired or which may even have been "thrust upon" him seems to have been a restriction to him. It is recorded of him that when his gardener needed to be reproved for his incompetence, Montefiore would go out and compliment him on some positive aspect of his work and then his wife would have to go out afterwards to the gardener to administer the needed reproof.[68]

Another Victorian, Friedrich Nietzsche, could see in this compunction about vigorous and even apparently negative behaviour, evidence of the enervating and debilitating influence of Christianity. In an attack on Wagner he says that he " . . . flatters every nihilistic Buddhist instinct, and disguises it in music; he flatters every kind of Christianity and every religious form and expression of decadence . . . " Also he writes, "Christianity has taken the side of everything weak, base, ill-constituted, it has made an ideal out of *opposition* to the preservative instincts of strong life."[69]

---

[66]S. Schechter, *Studies in Judaism,* vol. 2, Philadelphia, Jewish Publication Society, 1908, p.171.
[67]W.R. Matthews, *C.G. Montefiore, the Man and His Thought,* University of Southampton, 1956, p.5.
[68]Lucy Cohen, *Some Recollections of C.G. Montefiore,* London, Faber & Faber, 1940, pp.150-151, pp.74-75.
[69]W. Durant, *Story of Philos.,* New York, Pocket Library, 1960, p.412, & F. Nietzsche, *The Anti Christ,* London, Penguin, 1974, p.117.

But how much did the Victorian picture of the "saint" owe to the Christianity of the New Testament? A great deal of teaching could be brought forward to match the virtues of the "saint" with the exhortations of Christ and his apostles, especially in the Sermon on the Mount and Paul's "Hymn of Love" in I Corinthians 13. But as soon as we open our ears to the crash of the overturned tables of the moneychangers in Matthew 21:12 the spell is broken and balance is restored to the Christian profile of the saint. Even if we say that "The scourge of small cords" used by Jesus in the account in John 2:15 is for use only on the "oxen and sheep" and not the moneychangers, we are still left a scene of violence which would distress and even disgust a person in the Victorian tradition of saintliness. Montefiore is very critical about this aspect of the attitude of Jesus to his opponents. He quotes the saying of Jesus "Love your enemies; do good to them that hate you" and then he adds in parenthesis "(yes, even O Jesus, upon the scribe and the Pharisee, upon the vipers and the children of hell)."[70] The remarkable thing, of course, is that even after all this denunciation by Jesus, we read in Acts 15:5 of 'certain of the sect of the Pharisees which believed' participating in the Church Council in Jerusalem and also in Acts 21:20, James says to Paul "Thou seest, brother, how many thousands of Jews there are which believe; and they are all zealous of the law." From this it would seem that at least some of the Pharisees were better able to stand the robust castigations meted out to them by Jesus than Montefiore was to read about them. Montefiore felt he had a great cause and he too had bitter critics and enemies whom he dealt with in his own "saintly" way. Would his cause have prospered more if he had been less inhibited in the display of "righteous anger"? No doubt his Liberal principles and ideals would have suffered in the process, but Montefiore's restraint left his less inhibited opponents with a tactical advantage.

The Voluntary Self-Sacrifice

> ... this voluntary self-sacrifice for others, is one of the greatest ennoblements of suffering – is an idea which we meet with in the New Testament and in the Stoics, but which seems absent from the Rabbis. But Liberal Jews can adopt and develop it from the sources where they can find it.[71]

This concept of voluntary self-sacrifice is a favourite theme for Montefiore and just before the statement above he associates it with "The supremest chapter in Isaiah – I mean the fifty-third" and quoting from John 15:13 he says "What can be finer than this? This is my commandment that ye love one another even as I have loved you. Greater love hath no man than this, that a man lay down his

---

[70]C.G. Montefiore, *Liberal Judaism & Hellenism,* London, Macmillan, 1918, p.108.
[71]ibid, p.178.

life for his friends".[72] This is moving on through the Victorian temple into its inner shrine, the place of "supreme sacrifice" as it has been called. Montefiore sees this as a more typically Christian theme than a Jewish one and in doing this he is perhaps overlooking all that has been written on the AKEDAH theme (which is brought out so well by Shalom Spiegel in his book "*The Last Trial*"[73]) and also the "Kiddush Hashem" theme of martyrdom which he mentions but does not develop.[74] But after saying this, it must be acknowledged that Voluntary Self-Sacrifice, tied as it is in Christianity to the basic doctrine of the Atonement, is central, whereas in Judaism it could be called peripheral. Especially is this so if we consider the criticism of Montefiore's position made by Achad Ha'Am in his essay "Jewish and Christian Ethics" in which he quotes the Jewish authority Raba as saying "Let the other be killed (sic. – s.b. "die), and do not destroy yourself. For do what you will there must be a life lost: and how do you know that his blood is redder than yours? Perhaps yours is redder."[75] Such criticism sems to drive Montefiore almost into the Christian camp on this issue until one remembers that he says that whereas the role of Jesus as an Atonement and as a Mediator is central for Christianity, these concepts have no place in Judaism.[76] So what at first seems to be a typically theological and specifically Christian theme, for which Montefiore renders thanks to Christian teachers, has to be seen in a different light. Here his phrase "and in the Stoics" in our opening quotation gives a hint of other tributaries than the Christian one which have flowed into his 'voluntary self-sacrifice' concept.

As a boy, Montefiore might have thrilled to the story of the 'Charge of the Light Brigade' as he read "Storm'd at with shot and shell, while horse and hero fell . . . into the valley of Death rode the six hundred." As a young student of Latin he would have read the story of Mettus Curtius "A Roman who devoted himself to the service of his country, about 360 bc by leaping, on horseback and fully armed into a huge gap in the earth at the command of the oracle." He would have read, in his Greek studies of Iphigeneia at Aulis where she offers herself as a sacrifice saying "For a light unto Hellas thou fosteredst me and I die – O freely I die for thee."[77] As a mature man of 54 he would not have been too old to thrill at the story of the heroic self-sacrifice of the explorer Oates who stepped out of the shelter of Captain Scott's tent to die in an Antarctic blizzard to seek to lighten the burden of his companions in their struggle for survival. Also Dickens' character in '*A Tale of Two Cities*' who says as he prepares to sacrifice

---

[72]ibid, p.115.

[73]Shalom Spiegel, *The Last Trial*, New York, Schocken, 1969.

[74]C.G. Montefiore, *Liberal Judaism & Hellenism*, London, Macmillan, 1918, p.171.

[75]*Achad Ha'Am*, Oxford, East West Library, 1946, p.134.

[76]C.G. Montefiore, *Papers for Jewish People XII, The Place of Judaism*, London, Jewish Religious Union, 1916, pp.19-20.

[77]Euripides, *Iphigeneia at Aulis*, London, W. Heinemann Ltd., 1966, p.133.

his life to save that of another "It is a far, far better thing that I do, than I have ever done" would be part of the Victorian's "mental furniture."

But there is another darker element in this concept of voluntary self-sacrifice which goes beyond even the physical and moral courage so admired in the Imperial days of Queen Victoria and beyond until the slaughter of the 1914-18 conflict gave a more sober and realistic view of war. This darker element is the voluntary bearing of shame and disgrace, dishonour and ruin, the very antithesis of the unfading glory predicted for the heroes of the Light Brigade. It is hinted at in Isaiah 53:6 where we read "the Lord hath laid on him the iniquity of us all" and in Exodus 32:32 where Moses stands between the Lord and doomed Israel and asks that, rather than see his beloved people perish, he should himself be blotted "out of thy book which thou hast written." Paul likewise says "For I could wish myself accursed from Christ for my brethren, my kinsmen according to the flesh" (Romans 9:3).

Instead of a glorious ascent into the undying fame of a martyred hero, this concept speaks more of an ignominious descent into shame and sadness, experienced not as a justly deserved punishment but as a willingly embraced penalty which will expiate others' wrongdoing, or effect their rescue. Montefiore's classical studies would introduce him to the story of the descent of Orpheus into the underworld in search of his beloved wife. During his visits to church with Mr. Page, his Christian tutor, he would have heard in the Apostles' Creed "I believe in God the Father Almighty . . . and in Jesus Christ . . . crucified, dead and buried, he descended into Hell . . . " and he may have heard the words of I Peter 3:18-19 which tell us that Jesus was " . . . put to death in the flesh, but quickened by the Spirit; by which also he went and preached unto the spirits in prison." Or he may have heard Paul's words in Ephesians 4:9 where he says of Christ that he " . . . descended . . . into the lower parts of the earth." We have seen that Montefiore rejected all the Vicarious Atonement and Penal Substitution concepts of traditional Christian theology, but we have also seen that there is a reference to this symbol of the voluntary scapegoat, this Jungian archetype of the venturer into the dark abyss, in the classical sources, as well as in Scripture.

A very interesting echo of this concept can be recognized in the doctrine of "The Descent of the Zaddik," or righteous one, which is referred to in the Kabbalistic book, The Zohar, which states "The Zaddikim go down to Gehinnom, to the sinners who are in Sheol to bring them up from there." This teaching is taken up in the writings of Yaakov Yosef of Polnoy as being to the effect that "The zaddik must know the taste of sin and must feel the pang of guilt, but he is forbidden to transgress in the full sense of that word, to enter directly into the depths. It must only be 'as if' he had transgressed."[78] This last proviso is to distinguish Hasidic mysticism from the perverted antinomian

---

[78]Dresner, The Zaddik, New York, no date, Abelard Schumann, p.200.

application of this teaching which was practised by the Sabbatians. But the very mention of the word "mysticism" calls to mind the very many references in Montefiore's writings where he disclaims any familiarity with, or any involvement in, mysticism. He told Lucy Cohen[79] "I am no good at mysticism – only respectful." But in an address given in America in 1910 he says " . . . Judaism is not necessarily opposed to mysticism – not opposed that is to all and every mysticism, but only to *some* mysticism."[80] As Montefiore was a careful and diligent student, this observation presupposes a knowledge of Jewish mysticism sufficiently extensive to distinguish between what is acceptable and what is not. Also when we turn to his article "A Justification of Judaism,"[81] published in 1885, we find that he actually mentions the Kabbala. Even his extended note on the term MUSAR[82] in his 1887 lecture on the Wisdom of Solomon which defines the term as instruction, "a deliberate moral intention" might hint at some knowledge of the Jewish mystical and ethical movement known as the 'Musar' movement. But we have only to look at the background of Montefiore's tutor in Rabbinics, Solomon Schechter, to realize that the Hasidic form of mysticism would certainly have arisen in Schechter's teaching of Montefiore, because Schechter himself was "the child of a Hasidic, that is, mystic family born in the little town of Focsani in Moldavia."[83] Some such mystical influence and specifically in the direction of the doctrine of "The Descent of the Zaddik," seems to be the most likely explanation of a very remarkable outburst from Montefiore in his pamphlet "Do Liberal Jews teach Christianity?"[84] in which he says:

> There is no better mud to throw at Liberal Jews than to accuse them of teaching Christianity . . . . Now the present writer is an especially good target for such attacks . . . . What a sinner therefore is he and what a dangerous sinner! He sins from a darkened mind: the worst kind of sin . . . . Now do any of us Liberal Jews recognize Jesus as our Master and Lord? . . . Not even I, the greatest and muddies of sinners do so.

Although his tone is ironic, the real pain behind the words is inescapable. Called from a tranquil affluence to descend into the dusty arena of religious politics by the formation of the Jewish Religious Union in 1902, Montefiore

---

[79]Lucy Cohen, *Some Recollections of C.G. Montefiore,* London, Faber & Faber, 1940, p.113, cf *Rabbinic Anthology, p.232,* for non-mystical concept of 36 saints who atone for their generation.

[80]F. Synagogue Pulpit, 11:6-7, 1910, p.80.

[81]C.G. Montefiore, *A Justification of Judaism,* Boston, Unit Review, Aug. 1885. p.8.

[82]C.G. Montefiore, *The Wisdom of Solomon,* Jews College Lit. Society, 1887, p.15 & p.27.

[83]Norman Bentwich, *Claude Montefiore & his Tutor in Rabbinics,* University of Southampton, 1966, p.3.

[84]C.G. Montefiore, *Papers for Jewish People,* XXV, London, Jewish Religious Union, 1924, pp.10-12.

was attacked and insulted by Nationalist and also Orthodox Jews for his Universalism and his Liberalism, and by those who resented his admiration of some New Testament teaching. Because of these objections, his reputation and honour and loyalty were questioned far more than if he had been morally or criminally at fault. This for Montefiore was a personal counterpart to the supreme sacrifice, the painful descent, and the symbolism which he would have gathered from many sources, not only the acknowledged Christian ones, would no doubt have helped and encouraged him in his own voluntary self-sacrifice.

The Prophet

> The impulse and duty of speech are sometimes borne in upon me . . . the prophet of old was moved to speak . . . the prophet was justified in the end . . . . Would that I had a voice that could penetrate into every Jewish home where apathy or scepticism prevails. I would urge all that latent power to join me in battle for the cause of Judaism.[85]

Montefiore has been called a prophet by Dean Matthews and by Chaim Bermant, and in an interview I had with Montefiore's daughter-in-law, he was referred to as a prophet, but this was in connection with his striking eyes. Others have referred to his voice, his commanding presence and his general charisma. But these comments seem to refer to his *qualities,* the kind we would associate with a seer, a mystical "foreteller" of the future, whereas in the quotation given above, Montefiore seems to have the other *"forth*telling" or reforming *role* of the prophet, who actually *shapes* the future, in mind. His desire to reach into Jewish homes generally, and to have his fellow-Jews join him in battle for the cause of Judaism, seems to envisage a role of 'national prophet' for Anglo-Jewry in order to bring about its transformation. Montefiore's concept of what was needed did not stop short at "cosmetic" adjustments to Judaism to make it more acceptable to the English milieu. Rather he looked for deep-rooted change, indeed he considered that Liberalism was by definition *radical* because in an address given in America in 1910 he uses the terms interchangeably saying, "Liberal Jews, or Radical Jews, or Reform Jews (whichever word you prefer . . .).[86]

There was, of course, a great deal of precedent for the ministry of a prophet, especially a national prophet such as Elijah, Elisha, Isaiah or Ezekiel, in Jewish history. But in Jewish thought the prophets had been succeeded by "men of the Great Synagogue."[87] But Montefiore might be thought of as looking to the example of John the Baptist as "a prophet who arose after 400 years of silence." If, however, we look more closely at the role Montefiore saw for himself, we could say that his thought would have been drawn to a more modern figure, an eminent Victorian, a graduate of his own university, who had changed the course

---

[85]*Great is the Truth,* Jewish Religious Union, London, 1905, pp.13-14.
[86]F. Synagogue Pulpit, p.111.
[87]*Pirke Avot,* 1:1.

of ecclesiastical history in the 19th century. This man was John Henry Newman (1801-1890) who although he saw his work as being part of "the stand which had to be made against Liberalism"[88] and led the Oxford Movement in its attempt to restore Catholic doctrines and practices in the Protestant Church of England, Newman yet had a message for Montefiore. Although Montefiore was at *the opposite pole* so far as beliefs and sympathies were concerned, both he and Newman faced the daunting task of reversing the course of history and introducing change into a religious body which was bolted and barred against change by inertia, vested interests, sentiment and deep-rooted prejudices. The astounding thing about Newman was that with only a degree "granted by courtesy of the examiners"[89] (as Geoffrey Faber puts it), an Oriel fellowship, the relatively humble rank of priest and his own magnetic personality, he changed the nature of the Church of England. It was said of his "Essay on Development" (1845) that "since 1845 the whole history of the Anglican Church is but the vindication of the principles contained in that epoch-making treatise" and "the fact remains that the Anglican Church now repudiates as an insult the appellation of Protestant."[90] This was a dramatic reversal in an institution which once held that the Pope was the AntiChrist[91] and whose 39 Articles of Religion condemned Roman Catholic doctrine with such epithets as "blasphemous," "dangerous" and "repugnant." Compared with such a mountain, it would seem that the United Synagogue, the Chief Rabbinate and the 13 Principles of Faith were a much smaller obstacle for Montefiore's faith to move.

Newman and his associates had published their "Tracts for the Times" and Montefiore and his associates published their "Papers for Jewish People" (see chapter 3). The "Oxford" or "Tractarian Movement" was precipitated by John Keble's sermon on "National Apostasy" in 1833 and the Jewish Religious Union was precipitated by Lily Montagu's article "Spiritual Possibilities of Judaism Today" in the *Jewish Quarterly Review* in 1899.

It is interesting that in a letter to Lucy Cohen[92] Montefiore says of his own frame of mind at the time of writing "I do not ask to see the distant shore." This is a fairly obvious allusion to Newman's hymn "Lead Kindly Light" in which he says "I do not ask to see the distant scene; one step enough for me." In the dedicatory volume "Speculum Religionis" presented to Montefiore in 1929 on the occasion of his 70th birthday,[93] Professor Albert Cock of University College, Southampton actually lists Montefiore alongside Newman in a select

---

[88]J.H. Newman, *Apologia Pro Vita Sua*, Longmans Green, 1904, p.25, also see Ch. 3 "Parallels between Jewish Religious Union & Tractarians."
[89]*Oxford Apostles*, G. Faber, Pelican, London, 1954, p.70.
[90]C. Sarolea, *Cardinal Newman*, Edinburgh, T & T Clarke, 1908, pp.34-35.
[91]Apologia p.33.
[92]Lucy Cohen, *Some Recollections of C.G. Montefiore*, London, Faber & Faber, 1940, p.133.
[93]*Speculum Religionis*, Oxford, Clarendon Press, 1919, p.200.

group of which he felt it could be said, "In such souls . . . we catch the clearest glimpses of . . . Eternal Life." This is obviously intended as a compliment, but some words of Dr. Sarolea, a Roman Catholic biographer and champion of Newman are relevant here. He could say in Newman's *defence* "He resisted heroically, tragically, in order to maintain himself in the *via media* . . . he practiced subtlety . . . not in order to join the Roman Church, but to remain loyal to his Church and to be saved the final wrench."[94] No defender of Montefiore would use such words to describe his subject. It seems that it is in this area of personality and character that the disparate results from apparently similar endeavours may be partly explained. Anglicanism is now more Catholic than Anglo-Jewry is Liberal and despite the many parallels between Montefiore and Newman (including Newman's descent from a Continental Jewish family named Neumann[95]), it seems that Montefiore lacked the qualities which are sometimes seen in those who are able to change religious and political institutions from within. One "reformer" in the political sphere once said "You can't make an omelette without breaking some eggs." It seems that Montefiore's very nobility of character would have held him back from the kind of compromises which sometimes ease the progress of struggling movements.

The Unordained Minister

The distinction between Priest (Cohen) and Layman has become for us meaningless and even objectionable.[96]

When the first service of the Jewish Religious Union was held on October 18th 1902, although the Union included "distinguished representatives of the Orthodox ministry" (who withdrew during the first two years),[97] the sermon was preached by Claude Montefiore who, although he had once contemplated joining the rabbinate, was nevertheless a layman. Eventually, when the J.R.U. constituted itself as a synagogue in 1911, Claude Montefiore once again preached the first sermon but Lily Montagu says that they started " . . . in the faith that the advent of a Minister, so urgently required and so prayerfully awaited, would not be long delayed."[98] The following year Rabbi Israel Mattuck was inducted by Montefiore as minister. Montefiore as a lay preacher had good authority for his ministry in Jewish tradition because the role of rabbi was essentially that of

[94]C. Sarolea, *Cardinal Newman*, Edinburgh, T & T Clarke, 1908, p.31.
[95]ibid, p.37.
[96]C.G. Montefiore, *Papers for Jewish People, XXVIII*, London, Jewish Religious Union, 1928, p.4. See Abrahams & Montefiore, *Aspects of Judaism*, London, Macmillan, 1895, p.v.
[97]C.G. Montefiore, *Papers for Jewish People, XXVII*, London, Jewish Religious Union, 1927, p.5 & p.14.
[98]ibid, p.25.

communal teacher and the role of "priest" or professional religious leader had effectively disappeared with the loss of the Temple in AD70. When eventually the Jewish Religious Union followed the example of most denominations and sects of Christendom in handing over the ministry to professionals it might have seemed a natural development, but it could also be seen as a retreat from the early ideals of the movement. This was certainly the case with regard to women's ministry because the Hon. Lily Montagu (herself a preacher) points out in her account of the Jewish Religious Union and its beginnings that the suggestion made in 1905 in the Jewish Religious Union committee that women might be allowed to preach was not implemented until 1918.[99] Montefiore did point out in his book *Aspects of Judaism* that the concept of an ordained ministry was a late development in Judaism, and this would imply that his own lay ministry was more in keeping with normative Judaism. But it is just possible that the developments in contemporary Christian Nonconformity were not without their influence. The Irvingite movement, whose church was in Gordon Square, in which the order of prophetesses was revived, was not so very far away from Montefiore's home in Portman Square. Montefiore spoke with admiration of the achievements of th Salvation Army[100] who also encouraged the ministry of women officers. He refers to the Quakers[101] and even the Christadelphians[102] so he would also have been aware of a very influential, though small group known as the "Christian Brethren" which emerged early in the 19th century and which, unlike the Salvation Army, discouraged women's ministry but had a unique view of professional ministry. Normally, as has been remarked, denominational ministry tended to evolve naturally from lay or unordained ministry to an ordained or professional order. Among the Christian Brethren, however, because of a teaching known as "Dispensationalism," which held among other things, that the original order of the Apostolic Church had collapsed "in ruins" and was beyond repair, ministry was on the basis of interdependent equality. This kind of approach, without the eschatological presuppositions associated with it, would have been very congenial to the early Jewish Religious Union ideal but it seems that for various reasons, conformity to the prevailing custom won the day. It is interesting, however, that in the eulogy of Montefiore given at his funeral by Rabbi Mattuck, the professional minister brought in to be the "leader" of the new Jewish Religious Union synagogue, he refers to Montefiore and not himself as "our leader" and "teacher."[103] In the very different circumstances of the ancient Sanhedrin, the

---

[99]L. Montagu, *The Jewish Religious Union & its Beginnings,* (Papers for Jewish People XXVII) Jewish Religious Union, London, 1927, p.27.

[100]Montefiore & Loewe, *A Rabbinic Anthology,* New York, Meridian, 1938, p.xxii.

[101]Lucy Cohen, *Some Recollections of C.G. Montefiore,* London, Faber & Faber, 1940, p.135.

[102]ibid, p.177.

[103]I.I. Mattuck, *Our Debt to C.G. Montefiore,* Lib. Jew. Syn., 1938.

dual roles of Prince (Nasi) and Vice-president (Av Beth Din) might suggest a parallel to the respective roles of Montefiore and Mattuck.[104]

The Mission of Israel

Another theme which will repay investigation is the impact of the 19th century missionary movement, in its worldwide outreach, on the thinking of Liberal Jews as they pondered the role of Liberal Judaism as a future world religion. Because of the considerable import of this theme, it will be dealt with more fully later on.

---

[104]S. Schechter, *Studies in Judaism II*, p.105.

Chapter Three

Parallels Between the Jewish Religious Union
& the Tractarian Movement

Similarities between the two movements have already been referred to, and when these are seen in the context of very real dissimilarities, they are especially noteworthy. Although these were both Reform movements, one was moving towards Liberalism while the other was moving away from it. One operated within a large religious body and could enlist the special interest of a special group (see the tracts addressed Ad Clerum), many of whom had been students under the Tractarian leader, John Henry Newman, whereas the other was working with a minority group whose "clergy" lacked the professional and academic homogeneity of the Church of England ministers (except for "Anglicised" Jewish ministers before 1914) who were recognizably in "order," notwithstanding their various conflicting party loyalties.

Despite these dissimilarities, however, and although the philosophies and motivations of Tractarians and Liberal Jews were *diametrically opposed,* the dynamics of both situations seem to have prompted arguments which were in some ways strikingly similar. Each group had to win acceptance for ideas which were either strange, or associated with an "ancient foe," or both, so a very difficult reversal of values was involved in both cases. The Tractarians wanted to re-introduce certain ideas and attitudes which had been discarded in the 16th century Reformation. The mass, the adoration of saints and relics, the confessional and many other matters which were antithetical to the ethos of the Reformed Church of England had to be rehabilitated. In the case of the Jewish Religious Union, certain basic features of Jewish life, such as the Sabbath, the dietary laws and the rules for personal status and marriage were considered to be in need of modification. Also certain ideas and teachings from Hellenistic thought, with its pagan associations, and many concepts from Christianity, with its associations in the Jewish mind with persecution and error, were to be shown to be not incompatible with Jewish essentials. In both situations, a formal declaration of hostility towards the "ancient foe" was incorporated in the basic documents of the respective movements, to reassure those who were to be persuaded. This element can be traced in books, sermons, speeches, letters, etc., but especially in the two series of propaganda tracts already referred to – 'The Tracts for the Times,' issued by Newman's Oxford Movement, and the 'Papers for Jewish People,' issued by the Jewish Religious Union. The alliteration in both cases, T.F.T. and P.J.P. may be coincidental and the format, of 215mm x 140mm for the Papers for Jewish People and 222m x 136mm for the Tracts for the Times may be only coincidentally nearly identical in size. Also the use of Roman numerals agreeing with the Roman numerals used in some of the 'Tracts' give the 'Papers' a similarity which may be only superficial. But when we turn to specific passages in the literature of the two movements, we find parallels which are certainly of interest. We could begin by considering the similarities between the article with which Lily Montagu sounded her rallying call to Liberal Jews, and an early article by Newman. Miss Montagu says in 1899:

> It is only by association that we can effectually enunciate the principle, that we are required to use in God's service all the gifts of mind and heart which he has granted to us, since it is a form of blasphemy to conceal or to pervert truth in order to render our service to God acceptable to Him. We who . . . are conscious of our great needs, must organize ourselves into an association to rediscover our Judaism, encouraging one another to reformulate our ideal. We shall be able to rally round us the discontented and the weary, and together we may hope to lift Judaism from its desolate position and absorb it into our lives. Together we must sift, with all reverence, the pure from the impure in the laws which our ancestors formulated in order to satisfy the needs of their age, and refuse to resort to hair-splitting arguments in order to re-establish a religion, which was originally founded on a basis of truth, dignity and beauty.[1]

If the Jewish Religious Union had been already constituted, and had been looking for an alternative text to express their aims, would they have been tempted by the following?

> We have good hope . . . that a system will be rising up, superior to the age, yet harmonizing with, and carrying out its higher points, which will attract to itself those who are willing to make a venture and to face difficulties, for the sake of something higher in prospect. On this, as on other subjects, the proverb will apply, 'Fortes fortuna adjuvat.'[2]

This was Newman's description of the 'Via Media' he advocated in 1839,

> . . . by which was not to be understood a servile imitation of the past, but such a reproduction of it as is really new, while it is old.[3]

This very phrase 'Via Media,' in its English form 'Middle Way,' appears in the title of Montefiore's pamphlet, "Is there a Middle Way?", which he wrote in

---

[1]Lily Montagu, *The Jewish Religious Union & its Beginnings*, London, Jewish Religious Union (Papers for Jewish People XXVII), 1927, p.2.
[2]J.H. Newman, *Apologia Pro Vita Sua*, London, Longmans Green, 1904, p.63.
[3]ibid, p.63.

1920.[4] Like Newman, he had to dismiss this 'gradualist' option as a forlorn hope, although, unlike Newman, he did not try it out first, perhaps because the "Middle Way" of his mother's Reform synagogue had already served as a negative model. Montefiore affirmed that what he offered was the "Only Way"[5] and Newman eventually said the same. Another interesting item is that early in the experience of the Jewish Religious Union, the support and advice of an acknowledged scholar was seen as being of great significance. Miss Montagu says, "In preparing our liturgy for the Sabbath afternoon services held in 1902, at Wharncliffe Rooms, we had the inestimable advantage of the advice of Dr. Israel Abrahams, reader in Talmudic (sic) in the University of Cambridge and then Teacher of Homiletics at Jews' College. It is impossible to exaggerate the value of Dr. Abrahams' assistance . . . ."[6]

This was in no way intended as a slight to Montefiore, for he himself says,

> The history of the Liberal Jewish Movement in London may be divided into two parts . . . the first part – the ten years from 1902 to 1912 – was the more difficult period, and it was in this period that Israel Abrahams gave us the most valuable help.[7]

Later in the same volume, Montefiore says that Israel Abrahams,

> . . . was a convinced adherent of, and a doughty spearsman for, Liberal Judaism. His Liberalism matured, deepened, sharpened with the years.[8]

Also he said of Abrahams,

> . . . by far the greatest English-born Jewish scholar of his age was an enthusiastic Liberal Jew.[9]

But Herbert Loewe, a disciple of Abrahams, and his successor at Cambridge, thought differently. He wrote,

> Abrahams was more a man of the Jewish Religious Union than of the Liberal Jewish Synagogue . . . . The Liberal Jewish Synagogue had his warm support but he played a much greater part in the Jewish Religious Union . . . he was a super-Jew . . . above party designations."[10]

---

[4]C.G. Montefiore, *Is There a Middle Way?*, London, Jewish Religious Union (Papers for Jewish People XXIII), 1920.
[5]ibid, pp.14-15.
[6]Lily Montagu, *The Jewish Religious Union & its Beginnings,* London, Jewish Religious Union (Papers for Jewish People XXVII), 1927, p.7.
[7]C.G. Montefiore, *Studies in Memory of I. Abrahams,* New York, Jewish Inst. Relig. p.LXIV.
[8]ibid, p.343.
[9]ibid, p.LXII.
[10]H. Loewe, *Israel Abrahams,* Arthur Davis Mem. Trus., 1944, pp.68-69.

A comparable situation can be seen on the Tractarian side when we consider the role that Dr. E.B. Pusey (1800-1882) played in its development. Newman says that when Pusey became "fully associated with the Movement" (in 1835 and 1836) " . . . He at once gave to us a position and a name . . . Dr. Pusey was a Professor and Canon of Christ Church; he had a vast influence," he "was one who furnished the Movement with a front to the world . . . he was able to give a name, a form, and a personality, to what was without him a sort of mob . . . ."[11] The leaders of the Jewish Religious Union would not have needed to express themselves in quite this way, but they would have recognized the sentiments described. Also when Newman 'crossed over his Jordan' and 'entered the Promised Land' of the Roman Church in 1845 and Dr. Pusey stayed behind in the Anglican Church, a further parallel suggests itself when we remember Herbert Loewe's remark that, "Abrahams was more a man of the Jewish Religious Union than of the Liberal Jewish Synagogue." In both cases the "hiving-off" process left the influential scholar behind. In Pusey's case this was literally so, but in Abraham's case also, although he joined the Liberal Synagogue, his traditional Jewish lifestyle would tend to make him less comfortable with the new regime, as Loewe suggests.

Newman's role as a polemicist was much more difficult and complicated than that of Montefiore and his colleagues in the Jewish Religious Union, and Newman's complex personality tended to add to the complication, but another parallel can be seen in the polemical tactics both used. Newman and his associates had to establish their bona fides as English Churchmen, which at that period involved showing hostility to Roman Catholicism, even though they hoped to *commend* certain Roman Catholic doctrines and practices to their fellow Anglicans. So we find the author of Tract for the Times No. 59[12] speaking of the "capricious interference of the Bishop of Rome" and in Tract 51 we read "If the State religion became Roman Catholic, it could not be our duty to conform to that, because we should thereby compromise some of the fundamental articles of our faith . . . ."[13] In Tract 57 the writer classes "the spirit of Popery" with "all anti-Christian corruptions."[14] Instances of this "anti-Roman" attitude could be multiplied from Tractarian sources but our concern is not with the language, of which Newman says in 1843 "the divines of my own church (C of E in

---

[11]J.H. Newman, *Apologia Pro Vita Sua,* London, Longmans Green, 1904, pp.38-39.

[12]*Tracts for the Times* (By members of the University of Oxford) Vol.11, pt.I, 1834-5, London, Rivington, 1840, Tract 59, p.5.

[13]*Tracts for the Times* (By members of the University of Oxford) Vol.11, pt.I, 1834-5, London, Rivington, 1840, Tract 51, p.6.

[14]*Tracts for the Times* (By members of the University of Oxford) Vol.II, pt.I, 1834-5, London, Rivington, 1840, Tract 57, p.13.

1843) . . . have ever used the strongest language against Rome,"[15] but with its significance and effect. In a letter to John Keble in 1840 he says, " . . . the very circumstance that I have committed myself against Rome has the effect of setting to sleep people suspicious about me, which is painful now that I begin to have suspicions about myself."[16] These misgivings are repeated when he made a formal retraction of his criticisms of Roman Catholicism in February 1843 when he says,

> Yet I have reason to fear still, that such language is to be ascribed, in no small measure, to be impetuous temper, a hope of approving myself to persons I respect, and a wish to repel the charge of Romanism.[17]

The psychological and ethical questions raised here are fascinating but irrelevant to the issue, which is especially pertinent to the analogy between the the two movements. Newman, in seeking to win sympathy for the Church of Rome, of whose " . . . high gifts and strong claims . . . and its dependencies on our admiration, reverence, love, and gratitude"[18] he could write, also saw the need to maintain his credibility as an Anglican by going out of his way to " . . . say against Rome as much as ever I could, in order to protect myself against the charge of Popery."[19]

Montefiore, like Newman, was also accused of being, at heart, in sympathy with the object of his communion's hostility. In his pamphlet, 'Do Liberal Jews teach Christianity?' he acknowledges that critics of Liberal Judaism accused them of praising and imitating Christianity and generally behaving in such a way as to promote Jewish conversions to Christianity.[20] On this subject of conversion Montefiore considered that although it was wasteful and absurd for Christians to try to convert Jews,[21] he also says, "Apart from the question of children, we ought, perhaps to prefer that a Jew should become a Christian [than an] atheist or an agnostic."[22] Indeed, he says, "In the deepest and biggest things of all, you are not severed from your Christian neighbour, but at one with him."[23]

This sort of statement, which can be found throughout Montefiore's writings, is bold and magnanimous but also very disturbing for anybody in the

---

[15]J.H. Newman, *Apologia Pro Vita Sua*, London, Longmans Green, 1904, p.124.

[16]ibid, p.83.

[17]ibid, p.125.

[18]ibid, p.34.

[19]ibid, p.34.

[20]C.G. Montefiore, *Do Liberal Jews Teach Christianity?*, London, Jewish Religious Union (Papers for Jewish People, XXV), 1924.

[21]C.G. Montefiore, *The Place of Judaism in the Religions of the World*, London, Jewish Religious Union (Papers for Jewish People XII), 1916, p.16.

[22]ibid, p.9.

[23]ibid, p.18.

mainstream of Anglo-Jewry who was used to seeing Christianity as a rival faith and a threat, even in peaceful times, to Jewish identity. It is not surprising then to find a balancing negative note being struck in the Jewish Religious Union literature as Montefiore and others seek to show that they too can attack Christianity. Apart from such outbursts such as that of N.S. Joseph in Paper III, 'Why I am not a Christian,' in which he calls the Christian doctrine of the Atonement an "unworthy, irrational and hateful doctrine,"[24] the attacks are fairly restrained and therefore fall short of the vigour of Newman's attacks on Rome. It does seem, however, that they serve the same purpose. To take some examples, in 'The Old Testament and its Ethical Teaching,' Montefiore suggests that the cruelties of the Inquisitors could have been derived from the New Testament,[25] and that John's gospel displays a hatred of the enemies of Christianity.[26] In 'Liberal Judaism and the New Testament,' Montefiore can speak of Matthew 25 as containing "doctrine from which we turn in horror" . . . "odious . . . an awful aberration"[27] and of "Jesus, on . . . his pity and love (which only stop short, with a truly human limitation, at his own critics and antagonists)."[28] Of St. Paul's teaching he says, among many complimentary things, " . . . there is so much which is for us so crude, so remote, so false, so unworthy of God, so valueless for ourselves."[29] It would no doubt be easy to match all these negative elements in Montefiore's New Testament criticism from other sources, but when they are compared with his own enthusiastic praises of Jesus and Paul, they do seem somewhat strident. Alerted by the Tractarian model, it is possible to posit an understandable motivation for these elements which goes beyond the desire for scientifically objective even-handedness. Thus we read in Montefiore's address, 'Old and New' of his interest in the " . . . great general mass of Jews with whom we *desire to keep in touch*,"[30] and in 'The Jewish Religious Union and its Future,' about his concern lest Liberal Jews should be *cut off by themselves*.[31] He felt that he was achieving his aim of refuting the charge of pro-Christian bias when he wrote in 'Liberal Judaism and the New Testament' of himself as, " . . . the man . . . who has . . . this one great satisfaction,

---

[24]N.S. Joseph, *Why I am not a Christian*, London, Jewish Religious Union (Papers for Jewish People III), 1908, p.8.
[25]C.G. Montefiore, *The Old Testament & its Ethical Teaching*, London, Jewish Religious Union (Papers for Jewish People XV), 1917, p.6.
[26]ibid, p.17.
[27]C.G. Montefiore, *Liberal Judaism & Hellenism*, London, Macmillan, 1918, p.106.
[28]ibid, p.108.
[29]C.G. Montefiore, *Judaism & St. Paul*, London, Max Goschen, 1914, p.138.
[30]C.G. Montefiore, *Jewish Addresses*, London, Brimley Johnson, 1904, p.152.
[31]C.G. Montefiore, *The Jewish Religious Union & its Future*, London, Jewish Religious Union (Papers for Jewish People XIX ed. 2), 1918, p.11.

that he has been criticised by the Jews for praising too much and by the Christians for praising too little . . . ."[32] He could also comfort himself with a statement made about him that "No one [was] further from Christianity" and that he was "bigoted and one-sided."[33]

The Problem of Leakage

Both the Tractarians and the Jewish Religious Union faced the reformers' perennial pastoral problem of seeking to move their sheep from one pasture to another without losing any as strays or stragglers. To very the metaphor, they had to "Break the vessel but save the wine," and this has always been difficult. The Tractarians sought to promote a dissatisfaction in their readers with the then-current state of the Church of England, so that those they had disturbed would go on to what were judged to be better things, in the judgment of the Tractarians. The obvious danger was that, because movement was easier to start than control, some of their readers and hearers would leave their Church altogether and join one of the Dissenting sects, or even head precipitately for the Roman Church. We therefore find the Tractarian shepherds hedging in the path of their sheep by blocking off tempting alternative exits from the old pasture to ensure an unswerving progress toward the desired destination. In Tract 51, the clerical writer, addressing himself "Ad Populum," takes up remarks made to him, "when I have been visiting you in your cottages."[34] His parishioners had asked "Why should not a man attend both the Church and Meeting . . . . Why should not a man be a Dissenter . . . ?"[35] The writer is quite firm with his flock. He writes, "Dissent is a sin"[36] and concludes that his parishioners should affirm "I am more safe . . . if . . . I continue a member of the Established Church."[37] In Tract 57, disparaging remarks are made about Lutherans, Presbyterians, Congregationalists, Independents and Baptists[38] and "Popery" is also included as an "Anti-Christian .corruption."[39] Baptists, Non-Conformists and Papists are condemned in Tract 61,[40] Tract XXIV, addressed 'Ad Scholas'[41] attacks

---

[32]C.G. Montefiore, *Liberal Judaism & Hellenism,* London, Macmillan, 1918, p.124.

[33]*Speculum Religionis,* Oxford, Clarendon Press, 1929, p.6.

[34]*Tracts for the Times* (By members of the University of Oxford) Vol.11, pt.I, 1834-5, London, Rivington, 1840, Tract 51, p.1.

[35]ibid, p.1.

[36]ibid, p.2.

[37]ibid, p.14.

[38]*Tracts for the Times* (By members of the University of Oxford) Vol.II, pt.1, 1834-5, London, Rivington, 1840, Tract 57, pp.8-12.

[39]ibid, p.13.

[40]*Tracts for the Times* (By members of the University of Oxford) Vol.II, pt.1, 1834-5, London, Rivington, 1840, Tract 61, p.3.

[41]*Tracts for the Times* (By members of the University of Oxford) Vol.II, pt.1, 1834-5, London, Rivington, 1840, Tract XXIV.

Wesleyans and Dissenters, Baptist, Presbyterians, Zwiglians,[42] Socinians, Independents and Quakers.[43]

Montefiore and his associates were faced with the same basic problem, but there were far fewer gaps in the Anglo-Jewish hedge and their strictures could be more narrowly concentrated. Montefiore did not see the Reform Synagogue as a viable option for real progressives, because in its 60 year history it had acquired a measure of de-facto recognition from and even similarity to the Anglo-Jewish "establishment." Like the Tractarians, the Liberal Jewish reformers brushed aside any suggestion that they were a major cause of "straggling" and presented themselves as the only solution to an already existing problem, although they would perhaps admit to articulating and bringing into focus what many were already feeling in an inarticulate and unfocussed way.

Montefiore deals with the general problem of "dropping out" by saying that the "drifters" ought to "remain Jews,"[44] and he uses the term "drifter" on pages 5 and 21 and elsewhere for those whose links with Judaism are dissolving. He is not very concerned about Christian conversionist work[45] (although he deplores it) because,

> the Liberal Jew is seldom converted to Christianity . . . the orthodox Christian conversionists admit that the Liberal Jew is a harder nut to crack than the Orthodox Jew, and . . . it has been said . . . of the present writer that . . . he is hopelessly far removed from the borders of Christianity.[46]

His strongest strictures, indeed, are directed, as one would expect, against "rival" groups who would most closely resemble Liberal Jews and would therefore prove most attractive to the "progressive" Jews he was seeking to attract to Liberal Judaism. He comments in 'Jewish Addresses' that some Jews " . . . find Unitarian or Theistic services more suited to their religious aspirations . . . ,"[47] and in "Judaism, Unitarianism and Theism" he asks the question, "Are Unitarianism and Theism, purified forms of Judaism?"[48] In

---

[42]ibid, p.7.
[43]*Tracts for the times* (By members of the University of Oxford) Vol.II, pt.1, 1834-5, London, Rivington, 1840, Tract XXV, p.3.
[44]C.G. Montefiore, *Papers for Jewish People XIX*, London, Jewish Religious Union, 1918, p.10.
[45]C.G. Montefiore, *Papers for Jewish People XII*, London, Jewish Religious Union, 1916, p.16.
[46]C.G. Montefiore, *Liberal Judaism & Hellenism*, London, Macmillan, 1918, p.83-84, N.B. Montefiore here ignores loss to both wings of Judaism through exogamy.
[47]C.G. Montefiore, *Jewish Addresses*, London, Brimley, Johnson, 1904, p.5.
[48]C.G. Montefiore, *Judaism, Unitarianism & Theism*, London, Jewish Religious Union, (Papers for Jewish People IV) 1908, p.3.

answer, he dismisses the Theistic churches as "creations of yesterday"[49] and in writing to Unitarians he asks " . . . whether Unitarians may not be regarded as a modification of Judaism as fitly as of Christianity."[50] To his own Jewish Religious Union constituency, however, when speaking of Unitarians and theists, he makes the very cutting comment, "It is not for me to explain or defend the separate identity and the justified separate consciousness of those who hold the essence of the Jewish faith, but not the Jewish name . . . ."[51] He is similarly scathing about his friends (but rivals), the Broad Church Anglicans. Speaking of a statement by Prof Cheyne, he says,

> Reform Judaism is urged to at least complete 'its meagre, because predominantly negative' character by 'the recognition of the central importance of the person of Jesus and of the New Testament'[52]

His sarcastic comment is " . . . many Christianities lie open to our choice. Omitting the minor divisions, are we to become Catholic, Protestant or Unitarians?" or "a revival of the old Jewish-Christianity of the first century?"[53] He goes on, "Broad Church Christians of different shades are now engaged in endeavouring with varying degrees of success to fashion their own Christianity; are we to join them in their efforts?."[54]

Tract XC and the Thirteen Principles

A quite unmistakable parallel between the Tractarian and Liberal Jewish literature, is that seen in Newman's famous Tract No. 90, in which he compares the 39 Articles of Religion of the Church of England with the Roman Catholic doctrines defined by the Council of Trent, and Montefiore's address "Enlarge the Place of thy Tent"[55] in which he deals with the 13 Principles of the Jewish Faith. Newman's situation called for such an exposition as he made in Tract 90 because he was advocating a position which most people considered to be specifically condemned by the 39 Articles which he had publicly sworn to uphold.

Newman said of Tract 90, "It is a duty which we owe both to the Catholic Church, and to our own, to take our reformed confessions in the most Catholic

---

[49]ibid, p.11.
[50]C.G. Montefiore, *A Justification of Judaism,* Boston, Unit. Review, Aug-Sept. 1885, p.14.
[51]C.G. Montefiore, *Enlarge the Place of Thy Tent,* London, Jewish Religious Union, Address 13.1.06, p.15.
[52]C.G. Montefiore, *Jewish Quarterly Review,* Vol. 1, London, D. Nutt, 1889, p.278.
[53]ibid, p.279.
[54]ibid, p.279.
[55]C.G. Montefiore, *Enlarge the Place of Thy Tent,* London, Jewish Religious Union, Address 13.1.06.

sense they will admit: we have no duties towards their framers."[56] His reason for this was that he felt that "... the great stumbling-block lay in the 39 Articles ... the doctrine of the Old Church must live and speak in Anglican formularies, in the 39 Articles."[57]

An answer to Tract 90 by "four Oxford tutors" summarizes the tract as "suggesting that certain very important errors of the Church of Rome are not condemned by the Articles of the Church of England" and they list the doctrines of Purgatory, Pardons, Worshipping and Adoration of Images and relics, Invocation of Saints and the Mass.[58] The controversy about Tract 90 and Newman's eventual secession to Rome need no detain us as the apparent analogy between the 13 Principles and the 39 Articles serves only to throw the two situations into sharp contrast.

This is very clearly shown in Montefiore's address to the Jewish Religious Union of January 13th, 1906, entitled, 'Enlarge the Place of Thy Tent.' Montefiore is not concerned to show that he is fully committed to the 13 Principles of Faith, because they do not have the significance in English State Law that the 39 Articles had for the Church of England nor have they the credal authority of the Anglican formula. Neither did a career or a reputation hang on the issue for him as it did for Newman. So Montefiore, instead of wrestling with his creed, as Newman did, makes instead a straightforward analysis in which he takes Principles 1-5, 10, 11 and 13 as the basis for doctrines of God and Man and their inter-relationship,[59] and Principles 6-9 and 12, which refer to Scripture and Law and the Messiah, he replaces by "That doctrine ... [which] is called the Mission of Israel."[60] Montefiore is looking on to an improved, purified and updated statement of belief and does not look back to the medieval creed of Maimonides as the supreme authority for his faith. His frank inconoclasm is in sharp contrast to Newman's style of argument.

In summary, it could be said that the events of the Tractarian Movement, which did much to shape the religious thought of the age into which Montefiore was born, and which left a continuing mark on the Oxford to which he came to study are, in a *limited* but interesting manner, reflected and recapitulated in his own Liberal Jewish Movement.

---

[56]J.H. Newman, *Apologia Pro Vita Sua*, London, Longmans Green, 1904, p.81.
[57]ibid, p.80.
[58]Walsh, S. *History of Oxford M.* , London, Church Association, 1899, p.193.
[59]C.G. Montefiore, *Enlarge the Place of Thy Tent*, London, Jewish Religious Union, Address 13.1.06, pp.8-9.
[60]ibid, p.13.

Chapter Four

Montefiore's Philanthropy
& Some Victorian Parallels

Recent studies in the religious and social movements of the second half of the 19th century, in which Montefiore grew up, throw considerable light on his high estimate of Christian teaching and his extensive involvement in philanthropic work and suggest a connection between these factors in his life. Kathleen Heasman, in her book based on her doctoral thesis accepted by the University of London in 1960, says:

> ... as many as three-quarters of the total number of voluntary charitable organizations in the second half of the nineteenth century can be regarded as evangelical in character and control. The greater proportion of these were formed in the decades immediately after the mid-century, many of them as a result of the revival of that time.[1]

The Christian religious revival referred to is that which is dealt with by J. Edwin Orr in a book based on his Oxford doctoral thesis in which he writes,

> In the year 1859 a ... movement began in the United Kingdom, affecting every county in Ulster, Scotland, Wales and England, adding a million accessions to the evangelical churches, accomplishing a tremendous amount of social uplift, and giving an effective impulse to home and foreign missionary activity .... Amongst the converts and products of the Revival were such outstanding men as Tom Barnardo, founder of Barnardo's Homes ... and a host of others of note. Out of this movement grew such organizations as the Children's Special Service Mission, the Salvation Army, the China Inland Mission, and a great number of missionary activities, home and foreign.[2]

A similar religious movement had been witnessed in America as recorded by Dr. Orr who says,

> In the year 1858 an extraordinary religious Revival swept every state in the United States of America, adding a million converts to the churches,

---

[1]K. Heasman, *Evangelicals in Action*, London, G. Bles, 1962, p.14.
[2]J.E. Orr, *The Second Evangelical Awakening in Britain*, London, Marshall, Morgan & Scott, 1949, p.5.

accomplishing untold good, yet being utterly free from the fanaticism which had marred earlier American awakenings.[3]

Dr. Heasman takes up the story at this point, when she describes the visits of Charles G. Finney from America in 1849-51 and 1858-59 and says of him that his visits,

> . . . probably had some influence upon the mid-century revivalists, since for the first time in this century revivalists urged their converts to take up social work, with the result that many societies for this purpose were formed.

She goes on,

> Evangelical influence in this respect was far wider than its own religious group. . . . Numerous people of no particular religious allegiance were persuaded to undertake social work by the pattern of life around them. Such work became regarded as one of the common virtues and was followed by most of those who looked upon themselves as responsible members of the community.[4]

This activity was not entirely 'de novo' because a great deal had already been accomplished by the "Clapham Sect" from the late eighteenth century and on into the nineteenth, but the mid-century revival had a special impact in the field in which Montefiore was especially active, that which was covered by the Jewish Association for the Protection of Girls and Women.[5] Doctor Heasman mentions that in 1758, the 'Magdalen Hospital' had been founded for "penitent prostitutes" and within its walls "cropped hair and her dismal uniform constantly reminded the prostitute of her wrong-doing."[6] She goes on,

> It was on these lines that the High Church sisterhoods started their homes in the 1850s. Houses of refuge were established in the towns for 'the immediate reception of such fallen women as, desirous of forsaking their sin, knock at the door for admission.'[7]

A completely changed approach arose later and Dr. Heasman says of the 'rescue' work,

> . . . it was the late fifties before any serious attempt was made to combat the evil, and then it was closely bound up with the mid-century revival. Those visiting in connection with the revival were astounded by the debauchery they saw; the revivalists often suggested rescuing these

---

[3]ibid, p.5.
[4]K. Heasman, *Evangelicals in Action*, London, G. Bles, 1962, pp.26-27.
[5]Lucy Cohen, *Some Recollections of C.G. Montefiore*, London, Faber & Faber, 1940, p.147.
[6]K. Heasman, *Evangelicals in Action*, London, G. Bles, 1962, p.149.
[7]ibid, p.150.

girls as a useful form of social work, and frequently the girls were among their converts.[8]

She then makes a contrast with the earlier work which makes a strong link with Montefiore's approach to this and many other human problems. She says,

> instead of waiting for the girls to call as had been the case with the penitentiaries, many were brought to the homes by people who had specifically sought them out.[9]

Montefiore said of this 'seeking out' that, "This redeeming activity was, I believe, a new thing – at all events as practised with the methods of the intensity of Jesus."[10] But if it was new in the first century, it seems from the records that it was also relatively new in the mid-nineteenth century and Montefiore's introduction to rescue work in 1885, when he was asked to interview two Jewish women at the London Docks,[11] was an introduction to this new, or renewed 'seeking' approach. W.E. Gladstone, although not an Evangelical, employed a 'seeking' approach in his 'rescue' work and his example would have influenced Montefiore. As Kathleen Heasman puts it,

> The more understanding and kindly attitude towards the prostitute, which had been introduced by the Evangelicals, became a common approach.[12]

There are other, associated aspects of this mid-century socio-religious movement which find echoes in the lives of Montefiore and his associates. Dr. Heasman refers to "preventive" societies which existed to "keep girls off the streets" and she quotes Ellice Hopkins as saying in 1880,

> The rank and file of those who pass through our penitentiaries are for the most part young girls . . . whose original fault has been nothing greater than unruliness, the idleness, the silly birdlike vanity, and reckless love of fun, that we sometimes have to contend with in our own girls, during the difficult ages of fifteen to seventeen . . . .[13]

This intelligent seeking to deal with the roots of moral problems, seeking to "build a fence at the top of the cliff, instead of providing an ambulance at the bottom," greatly promoted work among young boys and girls such as was carried on by Montefiore's disciples, Lily Montagu and Basil Henriques. The National Vigilance Association was formed in 1885 with an Evangelical, W.A. Coote as its secretary and its work was also "preventive" in that it worked to suppress the

---

[8]ibid, pp.150-151.
[9]ibid, p.151.
[10]C.G. Montefiore, *Religious Teaching of Jesus*, London, Macmillan, 1910, p.55.
[11]Lucy Cohen, *Some Recollections of C.G. Montefiore*, London, Faber & Faber, 1940, p.69.
[12]K. Heasman, *Evangelicals in Action*, London, G. Bles, 1962, p.167.
[13]ibid, p.158.

brothels to which young girls were taken. This effort was later extended to action against the white slave traffic through Coote's organizing of an international conference in 1899 which eventually led to action at the League of Nations[14] in which Montefiore's Jewish Association was involved.[15] Another "preventative" measure was the "White Cross League," founded in 1883, which, with other similar groups sought to encourage men to,

> ...treat all women with respect and to endeavour to protect them from wrong and degradation ... and to use every possible means to fulfill the command 'to keep thyself pure.'[16]

This further insight into the aspirations of some in Montefiore's generation helps to set in context his own chivalrous attitude to women of whom he says,

> Perhaps it is – and was ... the noble women I have known who have most kept me a believer.... I have been privileged to know several well, of whom for beauty of mind and soul and heart I have felt unworthy to black their boots....[17]

An interesting note on the role of women in the sort of philanthropy practised by Montefiore is made by Dr. Heasman, who writes,

> The women's movement of the second half of the nineteenth century played an important part in recruiting workers for such societies.... Indirectly the movement inspired many middle-class women with the desire for emancipation, and so helped to swell the numbers of voluntary part-time workers.... Male social workers were not nearly so numerous. They were usually persons of considerable wealth and almost always held positions of control.[18]

It is easy to fit Montefiore and his Jewish Association workers into this pattern but on reflection, there is even an echo of the Jewish Religious Union here. Lily Montagu refers to "the principle of sex equality established since the beginning of our movement" and this reference, together with her thinly veiled indignation at a "thirteen years' delay" in accepting a 1905 suggestion that women should be permitted "to read in the synagogue" seem to align her with the "women's movement."[19] But when she refers to her own *priority* (graciously acknowleged by Montefiore) in initiating the Jewish Religious Union, "the forward

---

[14]ibid, p.166.
[15]Lucy Cohen, *Some Recollections of C.G. Montefiore*, London, Faber & Faber, 1940, p.147.
[16]K. Heasman, *Evangelicals in Action*, London, G. Bles, 1962, p.162.
[17]Lucy Cohen, *Some Recollections of C.G. Montefiore*, London, Faber & Faber, 1940, p.109.
[18]Heasman p.11.
[19]Lily Montagu, *The Jewish Religious Union & its Beginnings*, London, Jewish Religious Union, (Papers for Jewish People XXVII) 1927, p.27.

movement I felt called upon to make,"[20] she has to acknowledge the *pre-eminence* of Montefiore. Of him she says "From that day – the spring of 1901 – Mr. Montefiore became the great protagonist in the Liberal movement in England."[21] Without discussing the relative gifts of Montagu and Montefiore, it does seem that the apportionment of recognized male and female roles, referred to above by Dr. Heasman as a feature of late Victorian social work, was reflected, in some measure, in the early history of the social commitment of Liberal Judaism in England, as well as in its synagogal pattern.

Having concentrated on the work of Heasman and Orr because of their insights into the effects of the mid-century revival on matters germane to the Montefiore theme, it is necessary to note at this point that the wider picture also includes the work of the Unitarian Social Purity Alliance (1874) and the Christian Socialism of the Broad Church anglicans and the Anglo-Catholic social work in London's East end. Dr. Heasman makes mention of all these elements in her work. Although both Heasman and Orr write from the Evangelical standpoint, they do give sufficient evidence to support their claims that the ethical and religious climate of the England into which Montefiore was born was very powerfully influenced by the mid-century Evangelical Revival. This is especially significant when it is remembered that Montefiore's natural base was London, of which Dr. Heasman says, on the basis of religious censuses of 1851, 1886 and 1902-3, that,

> ... just under half the total population of London attended a place of worship of which probably as many as three-quarters were Evangelicals in the terms of our definition.[22]

The definition referred to is,

> The term evangelical is usually used to describe those Protestants who believe that the essential part of the Gospel consists in salvation by faith through the atoning death of Christ.[23]

Montefiore was familiar with several other types of Christianity, but if his comments on Christianity often presupposed this type, rather than the Broad Church or Anglo-Catholic positions of his Oxford mentors, it is probably due to impressions gained in his lifelong experience of the London scene. These impressions were of course reinforced by the internal tradition of caring charitable work within the Jewish Community, in work in which members of Montefiore's class occupied positions of leadership that were by no means sinecures. They led such bodies as The Jewish Board of Guardians, The Jews Free School, The United Synagogue and various Sephardi charities, etc.

---

[20]ibid, p.3.
[21]ibid, p.3.
[22]K. Heasman, *Evangelicals in Action,* London, G. Bles, 1962, p.18.
[23]ibid, p.15.

Chapter Five

The Question of Scriptural Inspiration

'Liberal Jews of all shades and varieties unanimously reject the doctrine of verbal inspiration. A doctrine of inspiration is substituted which, in the first place, allows for a human element of error and inadequacy, and in the second place, restricts the divine element in extent as well as in degree.' 'That is inspired and divine in the Bible which is original and good and true; that is purely human which was never good and was never true.'[1]

As we have seen from Lucy Cohen's reference to Montefiore's aspirations, while still in his twenties, for a renewed and rejuvenated Judaism,[2] the urge to bring about a further radical reform in his native Judaism was a powerful factor in the thinking of his young Reform Jew. But according to his son Leonard, at the Berkeley St. Reform synagogue where Montefiore was brought up, "Mr. Marks taught the verbal inspiration of the Pentateuch. He did not aim at or desire any doctrinal adjustment."[3] Whether this was affirmed by the speaker or inferred by the hearers, the resulting impression was clearly one favourable to verbal inspiration. It is important to notice the connection between "the verbal inspiration of the Pentateuch" and the precluding of "any doctrinal adjustment," because Montefiore himself makes this very same point in a tract on 'The Jewish Religious Union and its Future,' in which he complains that, "The written word remains: it is the same for all ages; it can never grow, expand, develop."[4] Of course Montefiore was as aware as anybody that a fixed literary deposit had never been an obstacle to writers prepared to "allegorize," "interpret," or even"supplement" revelation (by means of pseudepigraphy). But these were not viable options for a man of his temperament and integrity. If a sacred deposit of professedly divinely inspired scriptures stood in the way of his desired object of

---

[1]C.G. Montefiore, *Liberal Judaism & Hellenism,* London, Macmillan, 1918, pp.5-6.
[2]Lucy Cohen, *Some Recollections of C.G. Montefiore,* London, Faber & Faber, 1940, pp.56-57.
[3]Stein & Aaronsfeld, *L.G. Montefiore, In Memoriam,* London, Vallentine & Mitchell, 1964, p.71.
[4]C.G. Montefiore, *Papers for Jewish People XIX,* London, Jewish Religious Union, 1918, p.13.

reform, then the challenge had to be met head-on, in an honest and straightforward way, with a full and transparent setting out of all the problems involved, with all their ramifications.

Strangely enough, the basic obstacle to thoroughgoing Reform presented by what Montefiore called "the traditionalists'" view of the Pentateuch as the "verbally inspired oracle of God,"[5] is described better even than Montefiore can do it, by his own arch-critic Achad Ha'Am, in his 1894 essay, "The People of the Book." After speaking about the dynamic influence of a flexible, growing literature on the life of a people, he then describes a very different situation by saying:

> . . . a 'people of the book,' unlike a normal people, is a slave to a book. It has surrendered its whole soul to the written word. The book ceases to be what it should be, a source of ever-new inspiration and moral strength; on the contrary, its function in life is to weaken and finally to crush all spontaneity of action and emotion, till men become wholly dependent on the written word and incapable of responding to any stimulus in nature or human life without its permission and approval. Nor, even when that sanction is found, is the response simple and natural: it has to follow a prearranged and artificial plan. Consequently both the people and its book stand still from age to age; little or nothing changes, because the vital impulse to change is lacking on both sides. The people stagnates because heart and mind do not react directly and immediately to external events; the book stagnates because, as a result of this absence of direct reaction, heart and mind do not rise in revolt against the written word where it has ceased to be in harmony with current needs.

> We Jews have been a people of the book in this sense for nearly two thousand years; but we were not always so . . . in the period of the Second Temple, heart and mind had not lost their spontaneity of action and their self-reliance. But this state of things did not endure. The Oral Law (which is really the inner law, the law of the moral sense) was itself reduced to writing and fossilized, and the moral sense was left with only one clear and firm conviction – that of its own utter impotence and its eternal subservience to the written word. Conscience no longer had any authority in its own right; not conscience, but the book became the arbiter in every human question.[6]

This is an over-statement of the case, and tends to minimise the great ingenuity of the rabbis who worked over the centuries on Bible, Mishnah and Gemara and who continue to work, in the case of the orthodox, within the limits laid down by the Jewish literary tradition. Having said this, however, this extract has to be acknowledged as a masterly statement of the problem of a "given faith" which, in different ways confronts the three monotheistic and "literary" faiths,

---

[5]C.G. Montefiore, *Jewish Addresses,* London, Brimley Johnson, 1904, p.139.
[6]Achad Ha'Am (born Asher Ginsburg) *Achad Ha'Am,* Oxford, East & West Library, trans. & Ed. L. Simon, 1946, p.59-60.

Judaism, Christianity and Islam, each of which had also a deposit of additional written law, whether Rabbinic law, Canon law or Islamic law. Achad Ha'Am's solution is a revived Jewish nationalism, which was completely unacceptable to Montefiore. The problem, however, is very much Montefiore's problem, and it will be necessary to examine his approach to it and his response to its challenge. If an everyday analogy can be used, Montefiore can be compared to a property developer contemplating the redevelopment of a city block, who is told that all the existing buildings are listed for preservation, and that in no way can any alterations be made to the building facades. Some developers would concentrate on interior remodelling, some would make discreet enquiries about "accidental" fires, but Montefiore was of the kind that would have to fight for a reclassification of the buildings, especially as he was convinced that his projected "redevelopment" was for the higher good of all concerned.

The challenge in the Anglo-Jewish community of "the written word" which "can never grow, expand, develop"[7] and its clash with the researches in the natural sciences, was not new in Montefiore's day and even pre-dated the publication in 1859 of Darwin's *The Origin of Species*. In 1858, Dr. Markus Kalisch (who was home-tutor to the young Rothschilds) published *A Historical and Critical Commentary of the Old Testament with a New Translation,* in which he says "The book of Genesis . . . is evidently destined to become the arena for the critical discussion of the whole ground-work of Biblical theology, and for the introduction of a new era in religious thought."[8] Making his own contribution to the discussion, he asserts, " . . . with regard to astronomy and geology, the Biblical records are, in many essential points, utterly and irreconcilably at variance with the established results of modern researches."[9] He dismisses scornfully the suggestions "that the days mentioned in the Biblical record of Creation signify periods of a thousand years, or of indefinite extent."[10] Kalisch's comments give a very valuable insight into the standpoint of the numerically small, middle-class Anglo-Jewish intelligentsia of the mid-nineteenth century. His series of commentaries were advertised on the front page of the *Jewish Chronicle* in 1858 and called forth a counterblast from Haim Guedalla (1815-1904), so they were of some significance in communal thinking. His position was not quite as radical as he made it sound, because anticipating Darwin's later contributions to biology, he denounced those who alleged that "mankind itself has passed through stages similar to those which mark the progress of the various orders of animals! . . . It cannot be surprising, that

---

[7]C.G. Montefiore, *Papers for Jewish People XIX,* London, Jewish Religious Union, 1918, p.13.
[8]M.M. Kalisch, *A Historical & Critical Commentary of the Old Testament with a New Translation,* London, Longman, Brown, Green, Longmans & Roberts, Vol.I, p.iii.
[9]ibid, p.52.
[10]ibid, p.6.

such premises led to the most monstrous conclusions ... that man is a developed animal."[11] The basic challenge to Biblical authority, and therefore inspiration, remains, however, on the grounds of his opposing the "established results of modern researches" to the "utter impossibility of a creation of even the earth alone in six days."[12] He felt then that he could say " ... there seems indeed to be no alternative left, but honestly to acknowledge the immense difference existing between the Biblical conceptions and the established results of the natural sciences."[13] But traditional interpreters did not give up as easily as this and the situation in Montefiore's day and even in some circles today is that one interpreter will say "The divinely inspired and infallible scriptures teach a six-day creation" and another will answer "No, the divinely inspired and infallible scriptures teach a creation emerging in six great periods, referred to figuratively as 'days'." Despite the confidence shown by Kalisch as to the approaching demise of traditional scholarship, it seems that Lyell and Darwin and indeed Einstein can come and go without finally disposing of the issue which so exercised Montefiore, that of a "written word [which] can never grow, expand, develop."[14] Even if the Creation issue were settled, there were a thousand other issues, historical, scientific and ethical which in Montefiore's view were amenable to normal argument, evidence and proof, which were being needlessly complicated and even confused and obscured because of the Damoclean sword of an inspired revelation hanging over the disputants. For Montefiore, the issue was not whether Creation was effected in six days or 6000 years but how this or any other matter could be discussed freely within the parameters laid down by an infallible revelation. Montefiore was aware that the rabbis taught that one who said "the Law is not from heaven" had no share in the world to come[15] and he was also well aware of the traditional view of Scripture, still held by many in Christian circles in his day, despite the influence of critical scholarship. He makes clear his rejection of this whole attitude of subservience to Scripture, whether Jewish or Christian, by saying:

> ... my point is that what differentiates Judaism from at least *most* phases and forms of Christianity is, first, that it is not dependent on the verbal accuracy of the statements contained in a book, and, secondly, that it does not include among its essential requirements a belief in dogmas built up out of supposed historical events, the exact nature and accuracy of which can never be convincingly ascertained. Judaism, or at all events, the newer or liberal Judaism for which I am contending takes

---

[11]ibid, p.36.
[12]ibid, p.13.
[13]ibid, p.18.
[14]C.G. Montefiore, *Papers for Jewish People XIX*, London, Jewish Religious Union, 1918, p.13.
[15]Montefiore & Loewe, *A Rabbinic Anthology*, New York, Meridian, no date, p.605, cf Mishnah Sanh., 10:1.

its stand upon doctrines which critical and historical research cannot affect or undermine.[16]

As so much of Montefiore's literary output and lifelong concern was taken up by the Scriptures, both Jewish and Christian, this statement is of considerable import. He was of course aware of extra-scriptural Christian formulas such as the 39 Articles and the Tridentine creed, but as both affirm scriptural authority he would feel that they confirmed his statement. As a pointer to the attitude of his "newer or liberal Judaism" to the Scriptures and their authority, it also has significance, especially as we have already seen that Montefiore associated mainstream Judaism and even the Reform Judaism of his youth with a belief in the verbal inspiration of the Pentateuch.[17]

Any study of Montefiore's writings will indicate his familiarity with the Biblical scholarship of his day, especially that of Protestant writers, but also that of Catholic writers such as Alfred Loisy (1857-1940). It would be inaccurate, however, to deduce from this that Montefiore's independent and uninhibited approach to the Scriptures and the rabbinical writings was something which had come to him as a completely fresh insight as he read the works of nineteenth century Biblical scholars. Montefiore's training in the evaluation of ancient documents came to him under the instruction of Benjamin Jowett, Master of Balliol College, Oxford, his tutor in Classics, who was renowned as an authority on Plato and Thucydides. In his Prolegomenon to the 1974 reprint of *A Rabbinic Anthology*, Raphael Loewe comments on "an inadequate feeling for history – a feature which seems to have been not uncommon among the 'Greats' of nineteenth century Oxford." Loewe feels that a "short-sightedness" acquired in his Oxford days could have inhibited Montefiore's understanding of the value of the Rabbinic achievements and also of the historical contexts of the Hebrew Scriptures. In his 1892 Hibbert *Lectures on the origin and growth of Religion as Illustrated by the Religion of the Ancient Hebrews,* Montefiore acknowledges his debt to German, Dutch and English scholars in his preface, but his main tribute is to the one whom he was always to refer to as his "Master," Benjamin Jowett, and a quotation from Jowett stands at the beginning of the book and Montefiore was to refer to its message again and again in his writings. Jowett says:

> . . . in all religions: the consideration of their morality comes first, afterwards the truth of the documents in which they are recorded, or of the events natural or supernatural which are told of them . . . some have refused to believe in religion at all, unless a superhuman accuracy was discernable in every part of the record. The facts of an ancient or religious history are amongst the most important of all facts; but they

---

[16]C.G. Montefiore, *Enlarge the Place of Thy Tent,* London, Jewish Religious Union, 1906, p.10.

[17]Lucy Cohen, *Some Recollections of C.G. Montefiore,* London, Faber & Faber, 1940, p.57.

are frequently uncertain, and we only learn the true lesson which is to be gathered from them when we place ourselves above them.[18]

Montefiore conflates the beginning and end of this quotation into the axiom that the reader must "put himself above the documents."[19] Obviously this could involve the danger of being condescending and patronizing, but this is not what Jowett or Montefiore are saying. Rather they are moving away from a pious or subservient approach that would seem to them anti-rational and instead they come to the documents as scientific observers, neither hostile nor subordinated, but alert. In his preface to *The Dialogues of Plato*, Jowett says of the Librarians of ancient Alexandria, " . . . there was an inclination to believe rather than to enquire."[20] Certainly the Librarians did not learn this credulity from their copies of Plato's 'Republic,' in which we read:

> . . . we cannot allow Homer or any other poet to make this stupid mistake about the gods, or say that Zeus has two jars standing on the floor of his palace, full of fates, good in one and evil in the other.[21]

> It will be for the rulers of our city, then, if anyone, to deceive citizen or enemy for the good of the State.[22]

We also read that "we must value truthfulness highly,"[23] but Plato's approach to Homer and the other poets (the theologians of his day, *qua* transmitters and interpreters of mythology) and his own approach to theological communication was, to say the least, pragmatic.

A similarly pragmatic note is struck in Thucydides' *The Peloponnesian War*, in which the great historian of antiquity says:

> In this history I have made use of set speeches some of which were delivered just before and others during the war. I have found it difficult to remember the precise words used in the speeches which I listened to myself and my various informants have experienced the same difficulty; so my method has been, while keeping as closely as possible to the general sense of the words that were actually used, to make the speakers say what, in my opinion, was called for by each situation.

> And with regard to my factual reporting of the events of the war I have made it a principle not to write down the first story that came my way, and not even to be guided by my own general impressions; either I was

---

[18]B. Jowett, *Dialogues of Plato*, Ed.3, Vol.III, cited by C.G. Montefiore, *Hibbert Lectures 1892*, London, Williams & Norgate, 1892, p.vi.

[19]C.G. Montefiore, *The Old Testament & its Ethical Teaching*, London, Jewish Religious Union (Papers for Jewish People XV), 1917, p.1 etc. etc.

[20]B. Jowett, *Dialogues of Plato*, Ed.1, Vol.I, Oxford, Clarendon, 1892, p.xii.

[21]Plato, *The Republic*, trans. H.D.P. Lee, London, Penguin, part 3 (Book 2), 1962, p.117.

[22]ibid, p.126.

[23]ibid, p.126.

present myself at the events which I have described or else I have heard of them from eyewitnesses whose reports I have checked with as much thoroughness as possible. Not that even so the truth was easy to discover: different eyewitnesses gave different accounts of the same events, speaking out of partiality for one side or the other or else from imperfect memories. And it may well be that my history will seem less easy to read because of the absence in it of a romantic element. It will be enough for me, however, if these words of mine are judged useful by those who want to understand clearly the events which happened in the past . . . .[24]

Here we have two of the most respected writers of antiquity, writing of two of the most sacred themes in literature, religion and national history, and speaking quite frankly, even brutally frankly, about the difficulties inherent in the production of such writings. Montefiore was immersing himself in such thought long before he began a serious examination of the Jewish and Christian critical studies of the Scriptures. When he did eventually engage in controversy about those Scriptures with traditional Jews and traditional Christians (both of which groups held, in their own way, to a doctrine of divine inspiration of Scripture), he found himself thinking of Jowett, the classical scholar. In the Hibbert Lectures preface already quoted, he says:

. . . how much would the world have gained if the investigation of religion and of the Bible had been always conducted from the point of view and in the spirit enjoined upon us by the Master of Balliol![25]

But what did "placing oneself above the documents" do to the approach of the serious student of the Holy Scriptures? Although Jowett's field was Classics rather than Biblical Studies, he did write an essay, 'The Interpretation of Scripture' in the very influential *Essays and Reviews* which was published in 1860 and condemned by the Church of England Convocation in 1864. Jowett says:

Interpret the Scripture like any other book. There are many respects in which Scripture is unlike any other book; these will appear in the results of such an interpretation.

Who would write a bulky treatise about the method to be pursued in interpreting Plato or Sophocles? Let us not set out on our journey so heavily equipped that there is little chance of our arriving at the end of it. The method creates itself as we go on, beginning only with a few reflexions directed against plain errors. Such reflexions are the rules of common sense, which we acknowledge with respect to other works

---

[24]Thucydides, *The Peloponnesian War*, trans. Rex Warner, London, Penguin, Book 1, chap.1, 1959, p.24.
[25]C.G. Montefiore, *Hibbert Lectures,* London, Williams & Norgate, 1892, p.xi.

> written in dead languages: without pretending to novelty they may help us to 'return to nature' in the study of the sacred writings.[26]

> The intelligent mind will ask its own questions, and find for the most part its own answers.[27]

Plato, who, as we have seen, could be very severe with the "divine" poet Homer, would be quite content to have his work examined in this intelligent fashion. Thucydides, who had only asked that "these words of mine are judged useful by those who want to understand," would feel that his work had found the very kind of reader for whom it was written. But Biblical writers, both in the Old Testament and in the New, regarding themselves not as creative writers or scholarly investigators, but rather as instruments of God's self-communication, had a very different estimate of their work. Jeremiah, speaking in the name of the Lord says:

> 'Is not my word like fire' declares the Lord, 'and like a hammer that breaks a rock in pieces?'[28]

Isaiah addresses his readers thus:

> Hear the word of the Lord, you who tremble at his word."[29]

The New Testament endorses and strengthens this high view of Scriptural inspiration and authority which sees Scripture as 'the word of the Lord' by saying:

> Above all, you must understand that no prophecy of Scripture came about by the prophet's own interpretation. For prophecy never had its origin in the will of man, but men spoke from God as they were carried along by the Holy Spirit."[30]

The strongest claim of all is made in the Pastoral epistles of the New Testament where we read:

> 'All Scripture is God-Breathed' (Theopneustos).[31] (cp ASV 'Every Scripture inspired by God is also profitable.')

These are very solemn and weighty words about the Holy Scriptures, and both Jowett and Montefiore would be familiar with them and would note them with interest, just as an archeologist would notice and record the prohibitions and

---

[26]B. Jowett, *Religious Thought in the 19th Century*, B.M.G. Reardon, CUP, 1966, p.315.
[27]ibid, p.319. (essay 'The Interpretation of Scripture').
[28]Jeremiah 23:29, N.I.V.
[29]Isaiah 66:5, N.I.V.
[30]2 Peter 1:20-21, N.I.V.
[31]2 Timothy 3:16, N.I.V., cp A.S.V.

solemn adjurations inscribed on a sealed tomb, as he entered the tomb. For the scientific literary critic, as for the trained archeologist, these pronouncements would be items for study, but would in no way be seen as directions and guidance as to the way in which study was to be carried out.

Because Montefiore's approach to Judaism and Christianity was essentially literary, rather than mystical, liturgical or historical, his presuppositions as he came to the study of the Hebrew Bible, the Greek New Testament and the Rabbinic writings are of great significance. Inasmuch as the Old Testament is not a single book but a series of documents compiled over a substantial period of time, whilst analogous considerations of chronology and development apply to the handling of these same Biblical documents in rabbinic sources, Montefiore's blindspot (or at least failure to focus) with regard to the historical dimension, must be considered a significant lacuna in his equipment for the task he undertook. From what has been seen regarding the influences at work on him whilst reading Classics at Oxford under Jowett, it seems clear that he came to a consideration of the Biblical critical studies of his own day with a mind that was already working along the lines of a critical approach to ancient writings. And as we have also seen, those ancient writings were themselves a model and exemplar in the matter of assessing the relative worth of received moral and religious teaching. Thucydides could invent speeches and Plato could censor Homer and could write:

> We must therefore neither believe nor allow the story of the dreadful ravages of Theseus, son of Poseidon, and Peirithous, son of Zeus, or any of the other lies now told about the terrible and wicked things done by other sons of gods and by heroes. We must compel our poets to say either that they never did these things or that they are not the sons of gods; we cannot allow them to assert both. And they must not try to persuade our young men that the gods are the source of evil, and that heroes are not better than ordinary mortals; that, as we have said, is a wicked lie, for we proved that no evil can originate with the gods.[32]
>
> ...'the truth is that God is good, and he must be so described' ....
>
> 'That is true'
>
> 'And what is good is of service and a cause of well-being'
>
> 'Yes'
>
> 'So the good cannot be the cause of everything. It can only account for the presence of good and not for evil'
>
> 'Most certainly,' he agreed.

---

[32]Plato, *The Republic,* trans. H.D.P. Lee, London, Penguin, part 3 (Book 3), 1962, p.129.

'Then God, being good, cannot be responsible for everything, as is commonly said, but only for a small part of human life, for the greater part of which he has no responsibility.'[33]

For a man committed to refuting the proposition that "Man is the measure of all things," Plato is obviously here running the risk of undermining his own position by substituting a Platonic God (or gods) for the Homeric one, but the basic logic of the argument that God is good and therefore only what is good can be attributed to him or associated with him, is an attractive doctrine. Therefore, although Montefiore, unlike Plato, and unlike the "legislating" rabbis, is not "founding a state" and although he sees no need for authoritarian censorship or theological coercion, he does, like Plato, insist that "divine inspiration" must not be used as a cloak to cover the introduction or the preservation of subversive or unworthy ideas. With more than an echo of Plato's arguments, he writes:

> So far as the Hebrew Bible has true religious and ethical value and greatness, so far will that greatness and value be unaffected by any fresh view of inspiration or by any denial of miracle. No miracle and no theory of inspiration can make a given utterance better than its contents. They can neither add to the excellence of that utterance nor diminish it. But, on the other hand, the old theory of inspiration can cause great trouble if it conflicts with our ethical and religious judgment. Nor can a miraculous tale bolster up a bad or an imperfect ethical utterance. To those who believe that God is the Source of Goodness, what is good is divine; the more good, the more divine. But we can never any more be induced to believe – and we are surely glad of it – that any conception or utterance is good and true and perfect because it is contained in a book which is alleged, either by itself or by any dogma or theory, to be inspired and divine. The authority of the good and the true lie in themselves. They carry with them their own credentials.[34]

To ensure that these principles will not be taken as applying to the Old Testament alone he later says:

> ... the New Testament is also a book, and thus falls under the rule of imperfection and incompleteness which all books must display.[35]

As a result of this seeking to adopt Jowett's doctrine of "placing himself above the documents," Montefiore felt free to say:

> The Liberal Jewish position is emancipating. It puts us upon a height. We breathe a purer and serener air.[36]

---

[33]ibid, part 3 (Book 2), p.117.
[34]C.G. Montefiore, *Liberal Judaism & Hellenism*, London, Macmillan, 1918, p.7-8.
[35]ibid, p.13.
[36]ibid, p.13.

However true this claim might be, Montefiore's "elevation" also put a distance between his own position and that of the traditional Christians, to whom his writings, at least in part, were addressed. As far as Jews were concerned, it could well be that, although few of his contemporaries might have been able to formulate their (non-doctrinaire) misgivings about his position effectively, the deeply ingrained sense of historical continuity, together with development that characterizes normative Judaism made them realize that Montefiore's views set him apart from themselves. A logical consequence of their general endorsement by Jewry could be that the future of the Jewish tradition and the transmission of faith and ethics as a continuum could be placed in jeopardy.

Section Two

MONTEFIORE'S APPROACH
TO THE NEW TESTAMENT

Chapter Six

Montefiore's Three Mentors

Mention has already been made of the tutors who prepared Montefiore as a youth for his role in the Jewish community and for education at University. Whilst at University, his character and worldview were deeply influenced by the one he came to call "Master," Benjamin Jowett, 'who was Master of Balliol College. But when we consider Montefiore in his role of would-be "prophet" to Anglo-Jewry, a personified "Guide to the Perplexed" to the Jews of post-Emancipation England, the formative factors which went to make him what he was, must largely be traced to three Jewish scholars, Solomon Schechter, Israel Abrahams and Herbert Loewe. From the time that he met Schechter in Berlin in 1882, till his own death in 1938, Montefiore was in close consultation with one or another of these three scholars. The Mishnah taught the principle "Provide thyself a teacher"[1] and as these men, in succession, taught Rabbinics at Cambridge University, Montefiore's provision was of the very best. This was made possible partly by the considerable affluence he inherited (£1 million from his mother and £456,000 from his father),[2] which enabled him, even as a young graduate, to engage Solomon Schechter, a fellow-student in Berlin, as his tutor in Rabbinics, bringing him over to England on his return. Although all three of these scholars, in their successive roles as consultant to Montefiore, were primarily approached as experts in Rabbinics, the nature of Montefiore's studies was such that they would have considerable influence on his New Testament studies, which formed so large a part of his work.

Solomon Schechter (1847-1915)

When Montefiore met him in Berlin in 1882, Schechter was in his middle thirties, a native of Rumania, from the little town of Focsani in Moldavia. From a Hassidic family, he had attended a yeshiva at Lemburg in Galicia, and only then gone on to a more modern Jewish academy in Vienna and finally to the Jewish "Hochschule" in Berlin. His impressions of Christianity, gained first in Eastern Europe and later in 19th century Germany, would be very different from

---

[1]Pirke Avot 1:6.
[2]Chaim Bermant, *The Cousinhood,* London, Eyre & Spottiswoode, 1971, p.318.

those of the two English-born scholars, Abrahams and Loewe. Schechter would have vivid memories of a surrounding Gentile ignorance and superstition, and anti-Semitism of both the primitive and more refined varieties. He would find very little to argue with in the assessment of Abraham Geiger, founder of the Berlin Hochschule, which stated that "Christianity . . . counts sand among its treasures."[3] He might, with Geiger, concede that Christianity held " . . . within itself a full, pulsating religious life,"[4] but would perhaps also concur when Geiger wrote " . . . I view Christianity as the adversary of great cultural endeavour."[5] It has already been pointed out that some Continental Jews, such as Karl Marx and Franz Rosenzweig, felt rather overwhelmed and even smothered by the all-pervasive influence of established Christianity in the surrounding social environment and an English Jew, used to a more tolerant and urbane religious climate, might find this feeling hard to understand.

Montefiore made full use of Schechter's scholarship and expertise in Judaism and expressed his gratitude very handsomely in the preface of his *Lectures on the Origin and Growth of Religion . . . of the Ancient Hebrews* (1892). He says:

> To Mr. Schechter I owe more than I can adequately express here. My whole conception of the Law and of its place in Jewish religion and life is largely the fruit of his teaching and inspiration, while almost all the Rabbinic material upon which that conception rests was put before my notice and explained to me by him.[6]

But the correspondence passing between Montefiore and Schechter at this time shows signs of a developing tension which later erupted in bitter and sarcastic statements from Schechter, which evoked hurt and troubled responses from Montefiore. It would be anachronistic and perhaps simplistic to see this as due entirely to a clash between Schechter's "Conservatism" and Montefiore's "Liberalism." There were personal factors involved, such as Schechter's embarrassment at receiving financial assistance from Montefiore. Montefiore writes in a letter dated November 25th, 1885:

> You must try to [see] that the mere monetary relation in which we stand to each other shall become less painful to you. I can, indeed, appreciate your feelings to the full . . . .[7]

Schechter had moved from London to Cambridge in 1890 where as Lecturer and later as Reader in Rabbinics he was greatly appreciated and from where he

---

[3] Max Weiner, *Abraham Geiger & Liberal Judaism*, Philadelphia, J.P.S., 1962, p.92.
[4] ibid, p.92.
[5] ibid, p.125.
[6] C.G. Montefiore, *The Hibbert Lectures 1892*, Williams & Norgate, 1892, p.x.
[7] C.G. Montefiore, *Letters to S. Schechter*, U.S.A., Lib. of Jewish Theolog. Seminary no.1.

was able to journey out to Cairo to rescue the literary treasures of the Geniza in the old synagogue at Fostat, in 1896-1897. He returned to become Goldsmid Professor of Hebrew at University College, London, but in 1902 left to become Principal of the Jewish Theological Seminary in U.S.A. During these twenty years in England, Schechter's articles were published by Montefiore in the "Jewish Quarterly Review" which Montefiore edited with Israel Abrahams. Montefiore put a very high estimate on Schechter's stature as a theologian. He wrote "You have theological capacity. No other Jewish scholar that I know of has it."[8] But he refused to believe in Schechter's emerging role as leader of a Jewish "counter-reformation" which was to be based on the reorganized Jewish Theological Seminary in America. He wrote:

> I am quite sure there is no orthodoxy which would receive you. You would be too original for any creed .... You may call yourself what you please, but to me you are a liberal all round.[9]

Although there is no date available for this letter, it seems to belong to the period just before Schechter's departure for America when Montefiore was hurt and shocked by Schechter's slighting of his teachings in a letter to the 'Jewish Chronicle.' In a letter to Schechter dated December 12th 1900, he writes:

> Considering all things, when and since you know that the doctrine 'Englishmen of the Jewish Persuasion' is my heart's blood doctrine, for which I labour and give my life, *you* might be more courteous than to call it a 'sickly platitude.'[10]

Although this letter bears the date 1900, it seems to refer to the "Four Epistles to the Jews of England," published in the 'Jewish Chronicle,' London, in 1901 and republished in *Studies in Judaism,* Second Series, 1908.[11] In these letters, as well as decrying the "Englishman of the Jewish Persuasion" ideal of Montefiore, he attacks borrowing "commentaries on our Scriptures from the Christians,"[12] "Christian bias"[13] and the Christian commentators' tendency to assert that "the old Testament is only a preamble to the New Testament."[14] Schechter was no mere Othodox Jewish reactionary, because he later personally appointed Mordecai Kaplan, perhaps the most radical Jewish teacher of the century, to be professor of Homiletics at his Jewish Theological Seminary, where for three decades he was "the dominant intellectual influence on the

---

[8]ibid, no.66.
[9]ibid, no.72.
[10]ibid, no.65.
[11]S. Schechter, *Studies in Judaism, Second Series,* Philadelphia, J.P.S., 1908, pp. 182-201.
[12]ibid, p.199.
[13]ibid, p.200.
[14]ibid, p.201.

students."[15] Nor was Schechter merely a narrow critic of Christianity; he made many friends among his distinguished non-Jewish colleagues at Cambridge. Norman Bentwich says of him:

> He wrote several essays bearing directly upon the Talmud and its relation to Christian teaching. He was the author of the article upon the subject in *Hastings'Dictionary of the Bible;* and in two studies he pointed out the neglect or misuse of the Rabbinical literature by Christian theologians.[16]

Bentwich's next remark is, however, very relevant to this study of Montefiore and Christianity, especially with regard to Schechter's influence on Montefiore. Bentwich continues:

> But he held that the time had not yet come for a Jew to write an authoritative life of Jesus from the Jewish point of view.[17]

If, therefore, Schechter's influence had continued as a decisive factor in Montefiore's approach to Christianity, it would seem that the *Synoptic Gospels* commentary (1909) and many related books, would never have been written. Schechter had brought with him to England a certain suspicion and distrust of Christianity, or perhaps Christendom, its established and institutionalized manifestation, which he had seen in Europe and saw again in England. He only felt free from it in republican America, where Church and State were separate. As Montefiore put it in a letter to Schechter in 1898:

> You think I am rather wrong in my interpretation of the actual facts about us; and I think you are. Our upbringing, life, environment, etc. etc. have been *so* different that this is perhaps inevitable.[18]

This period of tension between Montefiore and the first of his three mentors, Solomon Schechter, marked a crisis in Montefiore's career. If he had succumbed to Schechter's pressure, his subsequent treatment of Christianity would have been much more restricted and perhaps would not have amounted to very much at all. As it was, the succeeding influences from his English-born mentors were much more congenial to his own keen desire to come to grips with the Christian documents and the one he called the "hero" of these documents.

---

[15]M. Kaplan, *Judaism as a Civilization,* Philadelphia, J.P.S., Introduction, A. Hertzberg, p.xxv.

[16]S. Schechter, *S. Schechter, Selected Writings,* Oxford, East West Library, 1946, p.26.

[17]ibid, p.26.

[18]J. Stein, ed., *Liber Freund: The Letters of Claude Goldsmid Montefiore to Solomon Schechter, 1885-1902,* Washington: University Press of America, 1988.

Israel Abrahams (1858-1924)

Here was perhaps the personification of Montefiore's "Englishman of the Jewish persuasion." Abrahams was born in England, loved cricket and although socially and financially he was in a different category from Montefiore, they shared an appreciation of the concepts and values of the educated and cultivated English gentleman at the turn of the century. Abrahams was also an associate of Schechter in 1885 in a group known as the "Wandering Jews" which included Moses Gaster, Israel Zangwill, Lucien Wolf and Joseph Jacobs. It is interesting to notice an early overlapping of the Schechter and Abrahams periods with the joint editorship of the 'Jewish Quarterly Review' (1889-1908) by Abrahams and Montefiore, Abrahams' involvement in the preparation of the manuscript of Montefiore's published Hibbert Lectures (1892), and his publishing, with Montefiore, of *Aspects of Judaism* (1895). Unlike Schechter, Abrahams threw himself enthusiastically into the launching of the 'Jewish Religious Union' (1902) which was the forerunner of the Liberal Jewish Synagogue. There is conflicting testimony about Abrahams' place in the Jewish religious spectrum and this is possibly very relevant to his own attitude to the relationship between the New Testament and the emerging Liberal Jewish movement. Lily Montagu, a co-founder with Montefiore of the Jewish Religious Union, speaks of:

> . . . the inestimable advantage of the advice of Dr. Israel Abrahams, Reader in Talmudic in the University of Cambridge and the Teacher of Homiletics at Jews College. It is impossible to exaggerate the value of Dr. Abrahams' assistance.[19]

In similar vein Montefiore writes:

> The history of the Liberal Jewish Movement in London may be divided into two parts . . . the first part - the ten years from 1902-1912 – was the more difficult period: and it was in this period that Israel Abrahams gave us the most valuable help.[20]

Later in the same volume, Montefiore says that Israel Abrahams:

> . . . was a convinced adherent of, and a doughty spearsman for, Liberal Judaism. His Liberalism matured, deepened, sharpened with the years.[21]

Also he said of Abrahams:

---

[19]L. Montagu, *The Jewish Religious Union and its Beginnings*, London, Jewish Religious Union, 1927 (Papers for Jewish People XXVII), p.7.
[20]C.G. Montefiore, *Studies in Memory of I. Abrahams*, New York, Jewish Institute of Religion, 1927, p.lxiv.
[21]ibid, p.343.

... by far the greatest English-born Jewish scholar of his age was an enthusiastic Liberal Jew.[22]

The period of Abrahams' fullest involvement with the Jewish Religious Union (1902-1912), however, is precisely that of the Union's more amorphous stage, when it still included, as late as 1909, ministers of the orthodox United Synagogue.[23] Abrahams had taught at Jews College (the seminary for mainstream Orthodox ministers) and his association with the Jewish Religious Union would not involve him in any danger of a formal break with the Orthodox community until the setting up of a separate synagogue by the Liberals in the 1910-1912 period. This historical background lends support to the statement by Herbert Loewe, a disciple of Abrahams and his successor at Cambridge, who wrote:

> ... Abrahams was more a man of the Jewish Religious Union than of the Liberal Jewish Synagogue .... The Liberal Jewish Synagogue had his warm support but he played a much greater part in the Jewish Religious Union ... he was a super Jew ... above party designations.
>
> Criticism appealed to him but he was essentially conservative ... generally [he] was orthodox.[24]

If both these testimonies are given due weight, it would seem that we have in Abrahams a man whose approach to the New Testament would be fair and open-minded but who would stop short of anything which would allow New Testament teaching to modify or even eclipse Rabbinic teaching, in the way one can see in Montefiore's *Synoptic Gospels* commentary, regarding Kashrut and the Sabbath.[25] Of Israel Abrahams then, it might be said that he was Liberal without being radical, and his stopping short of the radical aims of Montefiore's prophetic vision of a "Judaism of the Future" which would synthesize Jewish and Christian elements, would justify Herbert Loewe's description of him as "orthodox" and "conservative," in the non-technical sense of those words.

Abrahams' influence on Montefiore's New Testament writings is much more marked than that of Schechter, because Montefiore's magnum opus, *The Synoptic Gospels* commentary, was written during the Abrahams period and it was originally intended that Abrahams' explanatory notes to the commentary would provide a third volume to the two written by Montefiore. As it happened, the first section of these notes was not ready till 1917, eight years after the 1909 publication of the commentary. The second volume of notes was published in

---

[22]ibid, p.lxii.

[23]L. Montagu, *The Jewish Religious Union & its Beginnings,* London, Jewish Religious Union 1927 (Papers for Jewish People XXVII), p.20.

[24]H. Loewe, *Israel Abrahams,* A. Davis Memorial Trust, 1944, pp.68-69.

[25]C.G. Montefiore, *The Synoptic Gospels,* London, Macmillan, Vol.1, 1927, p.64 & p.131.

1924, three years before the 1927 second edition of the commentary, but it was possible to include in the 1927 edition an article on the "'Am ha'Aretz," written just before Abrahams' death in 1925.

The hiatus between the publication of Montefiore's commentary and Abrahams' associated but separately published notes raises interesting questions. Montefiore was satisfied that "Dr. Abrahams . . . was unavoidably prevented from carrying out his original intention"[26] of submitting his notes on the Synoptics for publication as Vol. 3 of the commentary. Abrahams himself wrote in his preface to his separately published notes, "The problems proved so many, so intricate, that I have found it beyond my capacity to deal with them all."[27] As Montefiore was working on the revision of his Synoptic commentary as early as March 1923,[28] it seems surprising that he and Abrahams could not come to some arrangement about joint publication of the second edition of the commentary. As it transpired, Montefiore's revision took him longer than the one year he envisaged in 1923[29] and Israel Abrahams died in 1925, one year after his own Gospel book was published. There is, however, another question raised by Abrahams' choice of title for his two books. Whereas Montefiore wrote a work about the Gospels, Abrahams wrote a book about *Pharisaism,* with the additional words "and the Gospels." Montefiore's reading of the Gospels did not move him to write a book about Pharisaism, but rather a book about Jesus and his teachings. Abrahams wrote as an heir of the Pharisees, but it would be very difficult to use this term of Montefiore, in spite of all his writings in defence of rabbis, Pharisees, Judaism and the Law. In his letters to Schechter he writes, in a rather sharp exchange:

> I have often defended your Rabbis etc. and have shown myself as a disciple of yours.[30]

Later he wrote:

> The Rabbinic religion is of course a mass of contradictions and antinomies.[31]

But in a letter about Dr. Michael Friedlander's book *The Jewish Religion* (1891) in which Friedlander writes:

> Eggs found in poultry are treated as meat, but must be salted separately

---

[26]ibid, p.viii.
[27]I. Abrahams, *Studies in Pharisaism & The Gospels,* Series 1, CUP, 1917, p.v.
[28]Lucy Cohen, *Some Recollections of C.G. Montefiore,* London, Faber & Faber, 1940, p.115.
[29]ibid, p.116.
[30]C.G. Montefiore, *Letters to S. Schechter,* U.S.A., Lib. of Jewish Theolog. Seminary no.65.
[31]ibid, no.68.

his comment is:

> May I *just once* say *how* Pharisaic (orig. emphasis)[32]

Montefiore was aware of sentences in his commentary which "criticize the teaching of the Rabbis," but he asks that "my estimate of that teaching [of Jesus] and of the teaching of the Rabbis may be considered as a whole."[33] This, however, would not solve the problem raised by the statements quoted above. Even if allowance is made for context, the heat of debate, the private nature of the correspondence etc., the fact still remains that a "whole" which refers to *your Rabbis* and uses the term "Pharisaic" in a pejorative sense is a different "whole" from anything that Schechter, Abrahams or Loewe would have produced. If a Christian were to speak of "*your* apostles" as if they were not also his own, or use the phrase "How *Pauline!*" in a pejorative sense, he might be able to point to compensatory statements elsewhere in his writings. Even so, his Christianity would be placed in a special category, and it seems that Montefiore's Jewish critics, and even perhaps his friends, would have to consider his Judaism as being also in a special category. Montefiore's view of the relationship between Christianity and Judaism, and his approach to both was different, therefore from Schechter's. Later it will be shown to be different from Herbert Loewe's. But an examination of Israel Abrahams' writings on Christianity will show that, in his own gentle and irenic way, Abrahams also dealt with Rabbinic Judaism and Christianity from a different standpoint from Montefiore's. Perhaps Montefiore could be seen as an *advocate* of the Rabbinic position, whereas Abrahams, with some reservations, *identified* with it. Montefiore was rather like an advocate who left the court room, after his defence, to go to his chambers, while Abrahams was like somebody who went down with the defendant to his place of confinement.

In his first book on Pharisaism and the Gospels, Abrahams says:

> Undoubtedly *a* (though not *the*) real Synoptic problem is: how to hold the balance truly between the teaching of Jesus on the one hand and of Pharisaic Judaism on the other.[34]

Abrahams eschewed any apologetic or controversial aims[35] in his work and even went so far as to show the rabbis and Jesus as somewhat complementary in their approach by writing:

> One might put it generally by asserting that the Rabbis attacked vice from the preventive side; they aimed at keeping men and women honest

---

[32]ibid, no.23.
[33]C.G. Montefiore, *The Synoptic Gospels*, London, Macmillan, 1927, p.670.
[34]I. Abrahams, *Studies in Pharisaism & The Gospels*, Series 1, CUP, 1917, p.vi.
[35]ibid, p.viii.

and chaste. Jesus approached it from the curative side; he aimed at saving the dishonest and the unchaste.[36]

But for all his "evenhandedness," Abrahams reveals himself, in his writings, as an heir of the Pharisees, one who would not shrink from calling himself a "Pharisee," at a time when this was a term of abuse, appearing in the Oxford Dictionary as a synonym for "hypocrite." Gentile writers such as Travers Herford took up the Pharisaic cause and defended it with great eloquence and enthusiasm, just as Montefiore did on occasion, but it was necessarily the advocacy of a 'friend,' but not the testimony of a 'chaber.' Schechter and Abrahams and Loewe spoke from within a Pharisaic experience, though each, of course, spoke from his own particular standpoint. Travers Herford the Unitarian and Montefiore the Liberal Jew, because of their measure of pro-Christian tendency (probably stronger in Montefiore than in Travers Herford), were not in a position to take up the *identity,* as distinct from the *cause* of the Pharisee. As Abrahams expressed it above, and as will be seen in any examination of the apostle Paul's teaching, it is a case of:

Jesus on the one hand and of Pharisaic Judaism on the other.

Montefiore's great enthusiasm was for "Prophetic" religion, which he saw reflected in the life and ministry of Jesus. Travers Herford had said that "Pharisaism is applied prophecy"[37] and Abrahams wrote:

. . . Pharisaism . . . effected a harmony between legislative punctiliousness as to detailed rules and the prophetic appeal to great principles.[38]

But for Montefiore the great prophetic teaching had *preceded* the 'Mosaic' system and Jesus was most attractive to him when he seemed to transcend, and shake free from, legalism, and sound forth truths reminiscent of the eighth century prophets. Abrahams, who could be quite gracious and appreciative of Jesus and his teaching, nevertheless was quite firm in subscribing to the spiritual authenticity of the position of the rabbis, who saw themselves in a succession which passed from Moses to Joshua, to the elders, to the prophets and finally to the men of the Great Synagogue.[39] The prophets were an important part of the chain of tradition which went back to Sinai, but the Pharisees saw themselves as living in a *rabbinic* era, not a *prophetic* one. Montefiore, taking his cue from his Christian contemporaries, saw the rabbis and their legalism as belonging to a bygone era. Abrahams and those like him, however, even though they might

---

[36]ibid, p.59.
[37]R.T. Herford, *The Pharisees,* Beacon Press, Boston, 1962, p.137.
[38]I. Abrahams, *Studies in Pharisaism & The Gospels,* Series 1, CUP, 1917, p.24.
[39]Pirke Avot, 1:1.

hold and express avant garde opinions, still saw themselves as heirs of the Pharisees, guardians of a rabbinic heritage.

There does seem, then, to be a different estimate of Pharisaism in Montefiore's writing, which is in contrast to that arrived at by Abrahams. The hiatus between the publication of the *Synoptic Gospels* commentary of Montefiore and that of the associated notes of Abrahams, already referred to, may indeed have been due to unavoidable difficulties of preparation. But notwithstanding this, the resulting disassociation between the two publications may well have been convenient for Abrahams. Where the unmistakable affinity of approach shown by Montefiore and Abrahams is seen at its best, is in the gracious and "humane" treatment of themes which had usually brought out the worst in Gentile and Jewish writers. Abrahams says in his Second Series:

> The humanism, which William Sanday so genially detected in me, derives primarily from C.G. Montefiore. His commentary on the Synoptic Gospels was the work of a pioneer from the Jewish side. Those of us who follow his method are proud to recognize in him a master and a guide.[40]

This approach, however, had its drawbacks. One of the Abrahams' readers, Professor A.T. Robertson, noted that Abrahams "felt no impulse towards a directly challenging style." Abrahams comments that this:

> was in this one case turned into an admission that I found nothing to challenge but accepted the very views which my book was designed to oppose.[41]

Another interesting instance of overlapping of the roles of Montefiore's "mentors," is found in the note in the 1927 edition of *Synoptic Gospels,* where we are told that the manuscript for Abrahams' essay on the "'Am ha'Aretz" was corrected by Herbert Loewe,[42] who is the last of the three collaborators of Montefiore to be considered in this chapter.

Herbert M.J. Loewe (1882-1940)

Because of Herbert Loewe's position as an orthodox Jew, the period of his co-operation with Montefiore serves to clarify even more sharply the attitude of Montefiore to both Christianity and Judaism. Schechter had been a fellow-student and fellow-Liberal with Montefiore, and his later development along a more conservative line, and the unfortunate tension between him and Montefiore tended to cloud the issues involved. Abrahams was a contemporary, and deeply involved in the first decade of the proto-Liberal group, the Jewish Religious

---

[40]I. Abrahams, *Studies in Pharisaism & The Gospels,* Series 11, CUP, 1924, p.viii.
[41]ibid, p.v.
[42]C.G. Montefiore, *The Synoptic Gospels,* London, Macmillan, 1927, p.viii.

Union, but for this very reason it would be difficult for him to emphasize too much his differences with Montefiore over basic issues. With Loewe, however, a distinct polarity in the Liberal and Orthodox positions which Montefiore and he held respectively, made it possible for the two collaborators to work together on a friendly basis, with each understanding the other's position very clearly, but with no compromise being attributable to either partner. This will be seen very clearly when the strictly Rabbinic material in the *Rabbinic Anthology* is considered, but even the book *Rabbinic Literature & Gospel Teachings,* which was prepared by Montefiore with Loewe's co-operation, is prefaced by the clear statement of Montefiore:

> Mr. Loewe . . . and I do not always look at the subject from the same point of view or in exactly the same way. He does not by any means always agree with me in my estimates and judgments, whether of the Rabbis or of the Gospels.[43]

Because this disagreement was quite friendly, and because Loewe saw his role as a scholar to be completely incompatible with any "partisan bias,"[44] the contrast between the views of Montefiore and Loewe must be given considerable weight when assessing the *objective* significance of Montefiore's departure from the traditional Jewish estimate of Christianity.

The occasion of the Montefiore-Loewe co-operation on the book *Rabbinic Literature & Gospel Teaching* was the appearance, between 1922-1928 of the four volumes of Strack and Billerbeck's *Kommentar zum neuen Testament aus Talmud und Midrasch.* This work was written by two Christian scholars (but mainly by Paul Billerbeck) and Montefiore calls it a "magnificent collection" and says that:

> . . . far the greater number of the citations [in his own book] can be found in, and were indeed taken from, Strack-Billerbeck's magnificent collection.[45]

Montefiore's quotations are, however, translated from the original, and not from Strack and Billerbeck's German.

It seems that the co-operation of Montefiore and Loewe in their major joint-publications was rather on the Talmudic basis of the Zuggoth or "Pairs" principle, in which each partner takes a different standpoint in what is sometimes called a "machlochet leshem shamayim," a contest in the name of Heaven. The result should be seen as a synoptic or complementary view of the topic being

---

[43]C.G. Montefiore, *Rabbinic Literature & Gospel Teachings,* London, Macmillan, 1930, p.viii.

[44]C.G. Montefiore & H. Loewe, *A Rabbinic Anthology,* New York, Meridian, 1938? p.lvii.

[45]C.G. Montefiore, *Rabbinic Literature & Gospel Teachings,* London, Macmillan, 1930, p.xv.

discussed. It is interesting to note that Montefiore's recurring formula "Mr. Loewe says . . . ," which introduces Loewe's often dissenting views is reminiscent of the Talmudic formula "Rabbi So-and-So says." Perhaps Montefiore also had in mind the Platonic Dialogues of his college days when he devised this format for these books.

The Strack and Billerbeck commentary sought to illustrate various New Testament passages by comparing and contrasting parallel rabbinic passages. Although Montefiore concedes that the quotations are accurate and possibly "more in the right than my [Liberal Jewish] spectacles enable me to see and to believe,"[46] he is provoked to "occasional quarrels with Strack-Billerbeck" as to the conclusions to be drawn from the Rabbinic quotations. But his "defence" of the Rabbinic position is clearly inadequate so far as Loewe is concerned. Time after time, Loewe is constrained to be "generously anxious to champion the rabbis,"[47] as Montefiore expresses it. Challenging Montefiore's assertion that "the teaching of Jesus appears superior to theirs" [the rabbis] Loewe asks:

> If Jesus's association with women was so novel, what about 'widows' houses? (Mark 12:40) You cannot have it both ways. If the Rabbis never spoke to women, how could they have influenced them to such an extent as to get their property? . . . . As to divorce, if Jesus was strict about divorce, so was Shammai. If he was tender, so was Hillel. How was he then, in a quite new and special way, the champion of women?[48]

There is quite an odd note struck in Montefiore's treatment of Strack and Billerbeck's comment on the New Testament statement in Matthew 5:43:

> Ye have heard that it hath been said: Thou shalt love thy neighbour, and hate thine enemy.

The Christian commentators say the command in Leviticus 19:18 enjoins love of the רע, one's neighbour, which may say meant only "fellow-Jew" to the rabbis. On this point and on two others, Montefiore says "the Christians win easily," thus using the language of contest and competition, which is far from compatible with is oft-repeated desire to avoid any suggestion of polemical or apologetic involvement. But what is of considerable concern to Loewe is that Montefiore seems to see himself free to cheer for whichever side impressed him, regardless of his own commitment. It is as if Montefiore were cycling alongside the River Isis in his Oxford days, sometimes cheering on his own Balliol College eight, and sometimes cheering for the rival boat-crew. Loewe and others like him, pulling at the oars in the Rabbinic boat, were entitled to protest at this incongruous behaviour. In the case of the רע (neighbour), and the גר (sojourner or guest), we read that:

---

[46]ibid, pp.xix-xx.
[47]ibid, p.47.
[48]ibid, p.47.

Mr. Loewe still tries to maintain that *ger* does not usually mean 'resident alien,' but 'sojourner' or 'guest' and that *rea'* in Leviticus 19:18 does not mean fellow-Jew only. His arguments fail to convince me: they are, I think, prompted by the intense *desire* that *rea'* in this verse as in 16 should, in the mind of the original writer, have consciously and definitely meant everybody, and so included the non-Jew.[49]

Instances of Loewe's defence of the Rabbis, in reaction against Montefiore's criticism of them, could be multiplied, but very often, as was noted in the Synoptic Commentary, Montefiore comes down on the side of the gospel emphasis and is critical of the rabbinic position. It is not surprising then that he is moved to comment that:

Mr. Loewe [is] generously anxious to champion the Rabbis, and to weaken any difference between their teaching and that of Jesus, if the teaching of Jesus appears superior to theirs . . .[50]

Montefiore even comments that Travers Herford:

. . . the distinguished Unitarian scholar is somewhat prejudiced in favour of the Rabbis.[51]

As will be seen when Montefiore's approach to the Rabbis is considered more fully, there is some indication of the opposite prejudice in Montefiore's case. There is a personal note struck in this connection quite often in Montefiore's writings which focusses on page 121 of the *Authorized Daily Prayer Book* of the United Synagogue (orthodox). There it is affirmed that:

For three transgressions women die in childbirth: because they have been negligent in regard to their periods of separation, in respect to the consecration of the first cake of the dough, and in the lighting of the Sabbath lamp.

Montefiore's dearly beloved wife, Therese, had died as the result of childbirth at the tender age of twenty-four and for Montefiore, this

. . . dictum in the Mishnah, which as I have often had occasion to observe, is still allowed to disgrace the Authorized Daily Prayer Book . . .[52]

was the voice of the Rabbis sounding out over the still, cold form of his beloved young wife and it horrified him. He says "one must not judge the Rabbis too

---

[49] ibid, pp.60-61.
[50] ibid, p.47.
[51] ibid, p.73.
[52] _____ *Auth. D.P. Bk*, Eyre & Spottiswoode, London, 1957, p.121, & C.G.M., *Rabb. Lit. & G. Teachings*, p.352.

harshly,"[53] but it is no coincidence that at this point he launches into a pointed comparison of the "long . . . composite . . . unedited . . . unexpurgated . . . naively and simply compiled" Talmud, with the "short . . . carefully written" Gospel, "so carefully written with the direct object of edification."[54]

Loewe could certainly sympathize with the depth of Montefiore's feeling and the close of his own introduction to the *Rabbinic Anthology* shows in what deep affection he held his older collaborator. But this is where Loewe's own comments on his own academic aim to be "objective," "free from partisan bias" apply. His vivid illustration of what he refers to as "congruence between the official and the personal views of the teacher" is very relevant to any analysis of Montefiore's position. He says:

> . . . while there is no reason why the Professor of Botany should not be a Buddhist, the Professor of Physics could hardly become an ardent member of the 'Flat Earth' Society and yet, in has University lectures, teach that the earth is round.[55]

Montefiore himself seems to see the incongruity of Travers Herford being "somewhat prejudiced in favour of the Rabbis."[56] Herford's remarks about Jesus ("himself was an Am-ha-aretz . . . ignorant of Pharisaic Halachic teaching")[57] and the Unitarian scholar's estimates of the relative merits of Christianity and Judaism do seem to indicate a bias which is out of keeping with a profession of Christianity. What Herbert Loewe seems to have found in Montefiore's attitude to Christianity was an incongruity which reversed the conclusions of Herford's position, but which was just as incongruous.

Whereas Montefiore could say "Jesus was not so far from the Rabbis, nor were the Rabbis so far from Jesus,"[58] Loewe affirms a very different position when he writes of:

> . . . the Jewish scheme of salvation by man's own efforts, helped by the divine mercy and grace.[59]

---

[53]C.G. Montefiore, *Rabbinic Literature & Gospel Teachings,* London, Macmillan, 1930, p.352.
[54]ibid, p.353.
[55]C.G. Montefiore & H. Loewe, *A Rabbinic Anthology,* New York, Meridian, 1938? p.lvii. N.B. Loewe, after Montefiore's death, re the problem of the "childbirth" prayer, quotes with approval D. de Sola Pool's translation, "It was held that for three reasons etc."
[56]C.G. Montefiore, *Rabbinic Literature & Gospel Teachings,* London, Macmillan, 1930, p.73.
[57]R.T. Herford, *The Pharisees,* Beacon Press, Boston, 1962, pp.206-7.
[58]C.G. Montefiore, *Rabbinic Literature & Gospel Teachings,* London, Macmillan, 1930, p.195.
[59]ibid, p.25.

It would seem that Loewe is determined to show that there is a genuine polarity or antinomy involved in any juxtaposition of Pharisaic Judaism and Christianity, which notwithstanding certain qualified statements of Montefiore, such as "Rabbinic Judaism is anti-Christian,"[60] is not fully acknowledged by Montefiore. This attempt by Loewe to clarify the border-line between the Jewish and Christian positions is something which had been tried by both Schechter and Abrahams from the conservative and liberal standpoints respectively, but, perhaps understandably, it was brought into sharper focus by Herbert Loewe, the orthodox Jew. The particular point at which this issue is dealt with most fully is in the discussion of Matthew 8:10. In that verse Jesus comments on the great faith of the Roman centurion who is able to believe in Jesus' power to work a miracle of healing, even at a distance. Montefiore feels that this shows:

> essentially trust in God ... it is not faith in Jesus ... is thoroughly Rabbinic ... is not off the Rabbinic line.[61]

Loewe challenges this by saying "I feel I am outside Rabbinic thought" (i.e., the Gospel teaching on faith is outside Rabbinic thought). He feels that undue importance is given to miracles and that faith in nearly all the relevant passages in the Gospels "means faith in Jesus." This brings the immediate retort from Montefiore:

> I do not agree; to Jesus at least, as *he* spoke them, they usually meant faith in God. – C.G.M.[62]

This is a sensitive point, because in all his plans to incorporate elements of Christian teaching into the "Judaism of the Future," Montefiore is faced with the challenge of the unassimilable element of personal devotion to Jesus, which he could not accept and which Loewe will not let him ignore. Loewe follows up this point by making a critique of Gospel faith in the Appendix 1 "On Faith," at the end of the book. Still commenting on Matthew 8:10, he writes:

> *Something new in Jesus' conception of faith.* Is it something new, after all? Is it not perhaps something very old and even superseded? ... one is right back again in Israel before the discovery of the Law ... the keystone is faith ... faith pure and simple ... it was a kindergarten teaching, needed for a kindergarten class. The Rabbis did not wish this to be given to those who had grown older, and had passed to a higher stage.[63]

Loewe therefore has brought matters into focus in this issue of the relative merits of Gospel teaching and Rabbinic teaching. Without any animus towards

---

[60]ibid, pp.160-161.
[61]ibid, pp.201-203.
[62]ibid, p.206.
[63]ibid, pp.377 & p.379.

his friend and collabortor Montefiore, and showing appropriate respect for Christians and Christianity as a whole, Loewe has taken up a clearly defined position which places him on one side with the Rabbis and Pharisaism, and Jesus and Christianity on the other. As Israel Abrahams had put it, it was a choice between "the teaching of Jesus on the one hand and of Pharisaic Judaism on the other."[64] This clarification of the situation was a faithful service performed for his friend, and it should have helped Montefiore in understanding his own position, but further examination of his development will show that it did not.

---

[64]I. Abrahams, *Studies in Pharisaism & The Gospels,* Series 1, CUP, 1917, p.vi.

Chapter Seven

An Analysis of Montefiore's New Testament Position

Historically there have been a number of classic Jewish responses to the New Testament and understandably Montefiore's readers have tended to classify him according to one or another of these stereotypes.

The Antithetical Response

One classic response is that made by the Jewish (Karaite) Polemicist, Isaac of Troki (1533-1593), who sought to polarize the Jewish and Christian positions by adopting a consistently negative position towards New Testament teachings, casing himself in the role of counsel for the prosecution. He says:

> . . . after a careful perusal of the Christian canon of faith, we have been impressed with the conviction that the authors of the N e w Testament have overlooked either intentionally or unintentionally, the real meaning and bearing of our original Sacred writings.[1]

As has already been pointed out, there is much in Montefiore's work which follows this pattern and this has led some to say of him:

> . . . in spite of certain supposed advances towards a due appreciation of the teaching of Jesus, there was none further from Christianity, no one more fixedly rooted in bigoted and one-sided Judaism, that he![2]

The Parallel Response

Another classic response is to see Judaism and Christianity as equally valid but distinct and mutually exclusive positions – parallel lines that never meet. This "Two-covenant" view is exemplified by Franz Rosenzweig (1886-1929) who said:

> We are wholly agreed as to what Christ and his church mean to the world: no one can reach the Father save through him. No one can reach the

---

[1]Isaac of Troki, *Faith Strengthened,* New York, Ktav, 1970, pp.227-228.
[2]C.G. Montefiore, *Outlines of Liberal Judaism,* London, Macmillan, 1923, p.325.

Father! But the situation is quite different for one who does not have to reach the Father because he is already with him. And this is true of the people of Israel (though not of individual Jews).[3]

Indications of such an approach have been detected by some in Montefiore's work. One has written:

Claude Montefiore was the first Jew to view Christianity entirely sympathetically. He felt no need to defend Judaism, to emphasize the defects of Christianity, or to write apologetically.[4]

The Christian Synthesis

The most famous exponent of a positive Jewish response to the Christian message is the Apostle Paul. He claimed to be still a Jew (Acts 22:3) and acknowledged that he was "a ringleader of the sect of the Nazarenes" (Acts 24:5 & 14), but he claimed also to worship "the God of my fathers, believing all things which are written in the law and in the prophets" (Acts 24:14). Paul then was advocating a synthesis of the Hebrew Bible and the new teaching of Christianity, but with the Christian teaching as controlling element in the synthesis. Some saw Montefiore as an advocate of such a position. Solomon Schechter said of Montefiore's teaching that it was not Liberal Judaism but Liberal Christianity.[5] Achad Ha'am said that the attitude to Christianity revealed in Montefiore's 1909 *Synoptic Gospels* commentary was that of one who had turned his back on Judaism.[6] Some Christians also saw Montefiore as having come over to the Christian side and were prepared to acknowledge him as one of their faith, despite his many protests to the contrary.[7]

The Jewish Synthesis

A Jewish response which is rather more rare than any of the foregoing seems to fit the evidence in Montefiore's case better than any of them. Traces of it can be found in the works of outstanding Jewish writers: it advocates a kind of synthesis, or perhaps a staged integration of Christian and Jewish elements, which sees the Jewish factor as the dominant one and the Christian factor as a preparation for Judaism. Both Yehudah Halevi and Moses Maimonides, while refuting the basic tenets of Christianity, could yet see a positive element in Christianity, which they saw as a kind of preparation for a universal adoption of

---

[3]N. Glatzer, *Fr. Rosenzweig, His Life & Thought,* New York, Schocken, 1961, p.341.
[4]L.H. Silberman, *Christianity through Jewish Eyes,* Cinc., HUC Press, 1974, p.93.
[5]Chaim Bermant, *The Cousinhood,* London, Eyre & Spott., 1971, p.318.
[6]L. Simon, Ed., *Achad Ha'am,* Oxford, East & West Library, 1946, p.131.
[7]W.R. Matthews, *Memories & Meanings,* London, Hodder & Stoughton, 1969, p.132.

Judaism.[8] Thus the New Testament would be seen as an introduction to the Old, and instead of the New Testament being an end in itself (with Christ seen as TELOS or goal), it would be seen as a means to an end, the end being Judaism and the conversion of the non-Jewish world to the Jewish faith. This would be easier for Maimonides to advocate, living as he did in a non-Christian milieu, than for his European fellow-Jews. Even in Montefiore's period, at the turn of the century, it called for some daring. But this was the basic presupposition which underlies his whole approach to the New Testament.

Montefiore did not need to destroy the New Testament, because he had a use for it. He did not envisage a continuing parallel existence for Christianity because he felt its days were numbered. Because of his negative prognosis for Christianity, he naturally had no use for a Christian-dominated synthesis. Rather, his great hope for the triumph of a "developed and purified Judaism" encouraged him to look for the emergence of a Judaism-dominated synthesis, which non-Jews would naturally warm to because of the inclusion of familiar "rescued" and re-oriented Christian elements, and which Jews could be taught to love. This will have to be considered later, under the heading "The Mission of Israel."

Montefiore's lifelong grappling with Christianity and the New Testament, his detailed and exhaustive analysis of the Synoptic Gospels, was not merely a labour of love in the interests of pure scholarship. His provocative championing of distinctively Christian emphases, when addressing his fellow-Jews, was not due to any mischievous or disloyal intentions. His criticism of distinctively Jewish emphases and exalting of Christian positions on the Dietary Laws and the Sabbath was not intended as a preparation for surrender to Christianity, but was rather seen by him as an essential preparation for taking over the Christian citadel.

A business man engaged in a desperate struggle for survival against a rival firm might denigrate his rival's products. But if he could foresee a future takeover of the rival firm, it would be in his interests to praise and protect everything in the rival establishment which he intended to incorporate into his own enterprise. He would of course not carry this course of action so far that it hindered the collapse of his rival and the looked-for takeover, but his attitude towards his rival's product, seen through the eyes of a prospective owner would tend to be benevolent. Such was Montefiore's attitude towards the New Testament, which, all things being considered, seemed to him a very good collection of mainly edifying literature.

---

[8]I. Heinemann, Tr., *Jehuda Halevi*, Oxford, East & West Library, 1947, p.121 & p.124. cf D. Hartman, *Maimonides, Torah & Philos. Quest*, Philadelphia, J.P.S., 1976, p.154.

Section Three

MONTEFIORE'S APPROACH
TO JEWISH SOURCES

Chapter Eight

The Old Testament & Rabbinics

Montefiore and the Old Testament

... few good books about the Bible are being produced by *Jewish* scholars, whether for students or the general reader. If you ask for helpful aids to the study of Amos or Proverbs or Exodus or Samuel or Job, you must chiefly be referred to books written by Christians. Of these there are plenty; of good books written by modern Jews there are few.

C.G. Montefiore (1906)[1]

Montefiore was brought up in the belief that the Hebrew Bible was of divine authority,[2] but he came to see the position of his childhood synagogue (West London Synagogue of British Jews, org. 1840) as transitional and untenable in the long term. Like the Reformed Jewish community on the Continent, it did not acknowledge the Oral Law or post-Biblical Rabbinic authorities as fully authoritative, (although it accorded them a qualified esteem) but unlike the more advanced Jews of the Continent, it still held to the inspiration of the Hebrew Bible. Montefiore likened their position to that of the Karaites,[3] the Jewish reformers who had sought from the 8th century onwards to reject Rabbinic tradition and base their faith on the Hebrew Bible alone.

Montefiore's youthful approach to the Bible was soon modified by his encounter with Benjamin Jowett, Master of Balliol College, Oxford, where he went to study. Jowett was famous as a philosophical scholar and exponent of Plato. Jowett did not, however, turn Montefiore into a philosopher. It was rather Jowett's subsidiary role as a Christian scholar and interpreter of Scripture which had the most telling effect on Montefiore. As outlined in the earlier chapter "The Question of Scriptural Inspiration," Jowett had called for a scientific and scholarly approach to Scripture, analogous to that used in the study of other ancient literature. As Montefiore points out in the quotation given above, this

---

[1]C.G. Montefiore, *Truth in Religion,* London, Macmillan, 1906, p.65.
[2]Stein & Aaronsfield, *L.G. Montefiore, In Memoriam,* London, Vallentine & Mitchell, 1964, p.71.
[3]C.G. Montefiore, *The Old Testament & After,* London, Macmillan, 1923, p.552.

was only possible if Christian study aids were used and this meant that Montefiore, who had accepted Jowett's thesis, was to see the Hebrew Scriptures, to a large extent for the rest of his days, from a "Christian" angle. As the attitudes of Christian exponents of critical Old Testament Scholarship were frequently coloured, even if subconsciously, by Christian presuppositions, their effect on Montefiore's outlook would be marked. This drew scorn from his one-time mentor, Solomon Schechter, who, in fairly obvious reference to Montefiore's writings condemned those who "need to borrow commentaries on our Scriptures from the Christians."[4] As an alumnus of the Berlin "Hochschule," Schechter naturally acknowledged the significance of the German Higher Critics, but warned against "a Christian bias" even in their work, which saw the Hebrew Bible merely as "a preamble to the New Testament,"[5] the effect of which would be to move Jews "from the 'Judengasse' into the Christian Ghetto."[6] Montefiore was hurt by Schechter's attacks, as seen in his correspondence with Schechter,[7] but continued to be guided by what he felt were the "best authorities." This consistently non-traditional approach to the Old Testament can be traced in *The Bible for Home Reading* (1 & 2, 1896/9), *Liberal Judaism & Hellenism* (1918), *Outlines of Liberal Judaism* (1923), *The Old Testament & After* (1923) and in *Introduction to Hebrew Bible* (1936). Montefiore's reaction to anybody who might accuse him of using "Christian" methods would be the same as that of any nuclear physicist who was told that he was using "Jewish methods" because he was following where Einstein had led. But despite the rational and scientific weight of Montefiore's argument, there was a lot to be said for Schechter's position, especially when Jewish survival and identity were given any measure of priority, as will be seen more clearly when Rabbinic Judaism is considered. It is perhaps helpful, in this connection to draw a distinction between the hardly disguised anti-Jewish animus of the leading German Old Testament Scholars, especially J. Wellhausen and P. deLagarde, and the Christian, but not anti-Jewish assumptions of e.g. S.R. Driver when commenting on e.g. Isaiah. Since the German scholars were the leaders of Old Testament Scholarship throughout the 19th century, and Graf and Wellhausen were responsible for the fully evolved Documentary Hypothesis, it was easy for Schechter to tinge the whole discipline with the stain of "higher antisemitism." His lead was then followed, especially by Jews who were sensitive regarding the Mosaic authorship traditionally accorded to the Pentateuch. But the "antisemitic" gibe was somewhat unfair when levelled at people like S.R. Driver.

---

[4]Solomon Schechter, *Studies in Judaism 11*, Philadelphia, Jewish Pub. Soc. 1908, p.199.
[5]ibid, p.201.
[6]ibid, p.200.
[7]J. Stein, ed., *Liber Freund: The Letters of Claude Goldsmid Montefiore to Solomon Schechter, 1885-1902*, Washington: University Press of America, 1988.

Montefiore and Rabbinics

Judaism could not become a universal religion together with its inviolate Law. It remains to be seen, now that Liberal Judaism has adopted an attitude towards that Law very different alike from that either of Paul or his antagonists, whether Judaism can, in practice as well as in theory, be transformed into a universal creed.[8]

Montefiore had a lifelong interest in Rabbinic teaching, as is shown by his engaging Solomon Schechter as his Rabbinic tutor in 1882, and his devotion of the closing energies of his long life to the *Rabbinic Anthology* (1938), and all of his many writings on Rabbinics in the years between. He could speak with admiration of the great joy experienced by orthodox Jews as they lived lives devoted to the observance of rabbinic regulations. He could argue cogently in defence of the rabbis against all comers, but all this did not make him a Rabbinic Jew. This is not to say that he was a fierce opponent of the Oral Law, nor that he was anti-Rabbinic, but rather that to him Rabbinic Law was part of the problem, rather than part of the solution he was seeking. As indicated in the quotation given above, Montefiore, learning from St. Paul, had come to the conclusion that the Rabbinic emphasis on Law, whether Biblical or Rabbinic, was incompatible with a universal creed, such as he envisaged the Judaism of the future to be.

As can be shown in his New Testament writings, Montefiore followed Jesus rather than the Hebrew Bible or the Rabbis in the matters of the Sabbath and the Dietary Laws. But as recent scholarship on Montefiore's attitude to the Rabbis has shown, Montefiore does not assess the rabbis according to their own canons. Rabbi Louis Jacobs writes:

Religion is not ethics ... it is in Halachah [legal teaching] that you find Rabbinic thinking crystallized, not in Aggadah [moral & ethical teaching].[9]

Because of the interpenetration of Halachah and Aggadah, this dichotomy cannot be pushed too far, especially when motivation and example in law-keeping are in view, but Rabbi Jacobs' point is taken.

Similarly, Dr. Joshua Stein writes:

Montefiore's policy with respect to the Rabbis of antiquity, was to judge them by the standards of his new faith. When their writings could be shown to fit the new pattern, he praises them. When Rabbinic attitudes are out of touch with the new doctrine, he chides them. Generally

---

[8]C.G. Montefiore, *Judaism & St. Paul*, London, Max Goschen, 1914, pp.145-146.
[9]Louis Jacobs, *Montefiore & Loewe on the Rabbis*, London, Lib. Jewish Synagogue, 1962, p.16 & p.22.

speaking, this pattern produces praise for *Midrash* and *Aggadic* Ethics and condemnation of *Halakhah*.10

Montefiore's continual juxtaposition of Rabbinic and Christian teaching, with frequent assertions that the teaching of Jesus is better, or his rather grudging admission that Jesus' teaching is matched by Rabbinic teaching "at its best," and very *infrequently* surpassed by Rabbinic teaching, shows that Jesus is used as a model and exemplar to evaluate the writings of the rabbis and not vice versa, as might have been expected.

10Stein, *C.G. Montefiore on the Ancient Rabbis,* Missoula, Scholars Press, 1977, p.1.

Section Four

LIBERAL JUDAISM

Chapter Nine

Liberal Judaism & Christianity

What the whole thing means, is not Liberal Judaism, but Liberal Christianity.

Solomon Schechter[1]

There were probably many of Montefiore's contemporaries who, without being as blunt as Schechter, would have harboured very similar thoughts about Montefiore's programme. But because of the special characteristics of the classic Christian position, specific denial of basic Christian beliefs, such as made by Montefiore on many occasions,[2] invalidates this thesis. On New Testament principles, a "crypto-Christian" on the Jewish "Marrano" or "Dönmeh" models, would be a contradiction in terms. Jesus said, "Whosoever shall deny me before men, him will I also deny before my Father which is in heaven" (Matthew 10:33). Even the most extreme "Liberal" in Liberal Christianity would probably hesitate to declare himself a "non-Christian" Christian and even Unitarians, though denying the divinity of Jesus, would not deny that they were Christians, as Montefiore so denied, on behalf of himself and his fellow Liberal Jews. But although Montefiore's Judaism can be shown to be non-Christian in the technical and theological sense, it does not give sufficient weight to the ethnic, cultural and even nationalistic elements in Judaism. Montefiore was aiming at a Judaism which would be a religious brotherhood, membership of which would not in any way hinder a full identification with a Jew's civil identity as an Italian, German, French or English citizen. Any aspect of Judaism which smacked of "foreignness" was a hindrance to this ideal. Even the recognition of a "Jewish" New Year's Day was suppressed and Montefiore consistently refers to Rosh Hashanah, the Jewish New Year, as the "Day of Memorial," and recognizes only January 1st as the New Year's Day for Liberal Jews. But the influx of new Jewish immigrants into Britain from Russia, after 1881, and the emergence of

---

[1]Solomon Schechter, quoted by R. Apple, *The Hampstead Synagogue*, London, Vallentine & Mitchell, 1967, p.38.
[2]C.G. Montefiore, *Papers for Jewish People XXV*, London, Jewish Religious Union, 1924, p.12 etc.

political Zionism, especially after 1897, seemed to shatter the Anglo-Jewish situation upon which Montefiore had looked with such hope and confidence.

Throughout this study it has been suggested that Montefiore's interpretation of both Judaism and Christianity has been largely shaped by his vision of a renewed and purified Judaism, which would incorporate the best of both faiths in a synthesis which would be found acceptable to the wider, non-Jewish world. It has been shown that Montefiore's pioneering studies in the New Testament and his application of New Testament insights to Liberal Jewish development can be seen as an assimilation of Judaism to Christian thought, not to help Jews to move more easily into Christianity, but rather that Christians should find Judaism more familiar and welcoming. This was Montefiore's contribution to the outworking of "The Mission of Israel."

The Mission of Israel

> ... the object of Israel's election is to disseminate throughout the world the knowledge of God.
>
> C.G. Montefiore[3]

I've caught a bear, but he won't let me go.

Old Hunting Proverb

Israel's obligation to bring the Gentiles to a knowledge of the God of Israel has been traced in the career of Abraham, in whom all nations were to be blessed (or bless themselves, Genesis 22:18), in the period of the prophets who saw Israel as "a light to the Gentiles" (Isaiah 42:6) and in many other periods throughout Jewish history. The rise of the rival faiths, Christianity and Islam, tended to inhibit Jewish missionary activity, which had previously been a marked feature of Hellenistic Judaism. Even after the rise of Islam, the story of the conversion of the Khazar kingdom in the 8th century shows that the Jewish interest in this field was not completely extinguished. The emergence of Reform and Liberal Judaism in modern times brought this missionary issue to the fore once again, because as the national or "tribal" aspect of Judaism (as Montefiore described it in 1882,)[4] is de-emphasized, the challenge of the wider Gentile world and its need becomes more pressing. But whenever this matter of Jewish proselytization of Gentiles is raised, its attendant threat of Jewish "destruction by dilution" is also raised. Traditional Jewish sources have been somewhat ambivalent on the matter of proselytes. Raba says in tractate Erub. 43b that when "the Messiah comes all will be anxious to serve Israel." In Av. Zar 24a R. Eliezer says "They will all become self-made proselytes in the time to come."

---

[3]C.G. Montefiore, *Liberal Judaism & Hellenism,* London, Macmillan, 1918, p.45.
[4]C.G. Montefiore, *Is Judaism a Tribal Religion?,* Contemp. Review, September 1882.

But in Yeb. 24b we red that "No proselytes will be accepted in the days of the Messiah" and in Yeb. 109b R. Helbo says "Proselytes are hurtful to Israel as a sore on the skin."

But to Montefiore's logical and uninhibited mind, *obligation* led in a straight line to *implementation,* and a great deal of his approach to Judaism and Christianity was with a view to launching just such a programme of Jewish proselytization of the Gentile world. Montefiore said in 1918:

> Liberal Judaism desires to exalt Judaism and to universalize it . . . wants to take Judaism into the big, broad air of the world.[5]

It is this encounter, or even confrontation, with the non-Jewish world which is the point of departure for any programme to implement the "Mission of Israel," but it has also proved to be a point of great danger for Israel down through the centuries. The nations may well be brought nearer to the God of Israel, but what would be the effect on Israel itself? Franz Rosenzweig, contrasting the roles of Church and Synagogue, says:

> "The synagogue . . . must renounce all work in this world, and muster all her strength to preserve her life and keep herself untainted by life. And so she leaves the work in the world to the church . . . the church, with unbreakable staff and eyes open to the world, this champion certain of victory, always faces the danger of having the vanquished draw up laws for her."[6]

Montefiore was well aware of this danger, and he was quite philosophical about the possibility that truths of Jewish origin might go on to conquer the world, while the name and identity of Judaism might be lost.[7] With his passion for "voluntary self-sacrifice," he would perhaps see a role for Judaism like that of the male bee, who is torn apart at the moment of mating with the Queen bee, who herself goes on to ensure the future of the species. Others were far from reconciled to the prospect of seeing Israel transformed beyond recognition by a vast influx of Gentile converts, who would become "the vanquished [who would] draw up laws for her" [Israel], as Rosenzweig felt had been the experience of the Church. Rosenzweig's vivid picture of the "indigestibility" of the multitudes of Gentile converts to Christianity was expressed thus:

> "The nations have been in a state of inner conflict ever since Christianity with its supernational power came upon them. Ever since

---

[5]C.G. Montefiore, *Papers for Jewish People XX,* London, Jewish Religious Union, 1918, p.10.
[6]N. Glatzer, *F. Rosenzweig, His Life & Thought,* New York, Schocken, 1967, pp.342-343.
[7]C.G. Montefiore, *The Old Testament & After,* London, Macmillan, 1923, p.568.

then, and everywhere, a Siegfried is at strife with that stranger, the man of the cross."[8]

Solomon Schechter, discussing the "missionary" vision of Liberal Judaism in his "Four Epistles to the Jews of England" in the Jewish Chronicle in 1901, is very deliberate in his demolition of Montefiore's programme, and Montefiore's hurt response in a letter to Schechter has already been noted.[9] Dismissing his contemporaries as not yet capable of missionary endeavour, Schechter goes on to list the pre-requisites of such a programme. There must be a "thoroughly and intensely Jewish" atmosphere among the Jews who would do this work, West and East must be enlisted, but he makes it clear that he looks particularly to Eastern European Jews to accomplish the task, which will be to ensure "that the whole world should become Jews, not that Judaism should fade out into the world."[10] Thus Montefiore's ideal of the "Englishman of the Jewish persuasion," proclaiming a "renewed and purified Judaism" with a substantial Christian element in it, is brushed aside in favour of traditional and "foreign" Judaism to which proselytes would have to integrate themselves in order to prove their bona fides.

"The Church of Israel"

The subject of converting Gentiles to Judaism had been aired in the *Jewish Quarterly Review* of 1894 by Montefiore in his article "Mr. Smith – A Possibility."[11] Israel Abrahams had followed with "Miss Smith: An Argument,"[12] in which he states that:

Judaism . . . has a direct duty to make converts

Oswald John Simon in the J.Q.R. of 1897 advocated the setting up of:

congregations of English people not of Jewish origin

who would be taught in English on Sundays by Jews,

the innermost faith of Israel,

---

[8]N. Glatzer, *F. Rosenzweig, His Life & Thought*, New York, Schocken, 1967, p.336.

[9]J. Stein, ed., *Liber Freund: The Letters of Claude Goldsmid Montefiore to Solomon Schechter, 1885-1902*, Washington: University Press of America, 1988.

[10]Solomon Schechter, *Studies in Judaism 11*, Philadelphia, J.P.S., 1908, p.185.

[11]C.G. Montefiore, *Jewish Quarterly Review 1894*, Vol.VI, p.100 ff.

[12]ibid, p.111.

but without Jewish rites or customs which would hinder the progress[13] of the congregants. Israel Abrahams heartily approved this scheme and Montefiore wrote:

> Such a Church of Israel, such a direct preaching of Judaism to the 'nations' is in full accordance with the highest conceptions of Judaism and its mission.[14]

The very obvious parallel between this scheme and existing Christian agencies did not escape H. Adler, who wrote:

> We justly deprecate Societies for the Promotion of Christianity among the Jews . . . should we not, by fostering the movement in question, commit a folly of like character?[15]

This raised another obstacle in addition to the danger of dilution by accession. Jewish involvement in proselytization would seem to be an endorsement of the practice. Complaints about coercion and inducements and unfair methods did not bar others from proselytizing, as some critics of Christian missions seemed to think. These complaints merely pointed to the need for better motivation and conduct in carrying on the work, and if Christian evangelists heeded these criticisms, it might even have the effect of prospering Christian proselytizing.

The theme recurs in *The Old Testament & After* (1923) and *Outlines of Liberal Judaism* (1923), with a climax to the discussion coming in the fateful year of Hitler's accession as German Chancelor in 1933, when the Jewish Religious Union published *Jewish Views on Jewish Missions*.[16] With the Nazi era just opening, this was perhaps the last opportunity to discuss this topic until its revival in recent times. The Jewish Religious Union had evolved into the Liberal Jewish Synagogue, and Rabbi I.I. Mattuck had become the effective leader of Liberal Judaism in England. The idealism of lay leaders such as Montefiore and Israel Abrahams had given way to a more pragmatic approach, and we find in Rabbi Mattuck's presentation "Why the Jews have no missionaries" a defence of the "passive witness" role of Israel as being an acceptable fulfillment of Israel's mission.

To Montefiore, this seemed like marking a virtue out of necessity,[17] a mere "sanctifying" of contemporary Jewish inertia in the matter of giving light to the world. To him, a universal religion placed a responsibility on its adherents to make it universally known. Far from despising the work of Christian

---

[13]O.J. Simon, *Jewish Quarterly Review 1897*, Vol.IX, pp.182-3.
[14]C.G. Montefiore, *Jewish Quarterly Review 1897*, Vol.IX, p.198.
[15]H. Adler, *Jewish Quarterly Review 1897*, Vol.IX, p.186.
[16]C.G. Montefiore & I.I. Mattuck, *Papers for Jewish People XXXI*, London, Jewish Religious Union, 1933.
[17]ibid, p.15.

missionaries in their universal outreach to the heathen, Montefiore admired them,[18] which is not surprising in one who would have been impressed by the great regard in which missionaries such as Livingstone and others had been held in the days of his youth. For him, the logic of the situation left:

> no escape from the argument that if Jews truly desired that Judaism, or the fundamental doctrines of Judaism, should, sooner rather than later, become the spiritual possession of all the world, they ought to go forth to the 'heathen' rather than sit still and expect the 'heathen' to come to them and 'learn.'[19]

---

[18]ibid, p.17.
[19]ibid, p.39.

Chapter Ten

Epilogue

When Montefiore conducted his discussion with Rabbi Mattuck about sending Jewish missionaries to the non-Jewish world, he was 75 years old and past the stage in his life when he could hope to launch this or any other major programme of action. Anglo-Jewry had changed, after the "Russian" influx of the 1880s, from being a fairly prosperous, settled and largely anglicised group, to become a more "foreign," unassimilated and rather "traditional" community. Violent Antisemitism had moved west into Germany and would soon overshadow even the worst excesses of the Tsarist cruelties. Jewish natinalism had revived, and although Montefiore saw this as a *cause* of increased Antisemitism, he yet records that Theodor Herzl had confessed to him that "it was antisemitism which had made him a Zionist."[1] As Liberalism in general began to wither, and war clouds began to gather, it is not surprising that world Jewry began to close ranks and look to its own resources to meet its needs, with an inevitable waxing of the Particularist stream and a waning of Montefiore's beloved Universalism.

Montefiore had many Christian friends, but his special "window" on the Christian world was his *London Society for the Study of Religion,* which he co-founded with the Roman Catholic scholar and mystic, Baron von Hugel in 1904. Fifteen of the original seventeen members were non-Jews and it was to this society in 1935 that he poured out his heart regarding the shattering of his life's dreams. Perhaps in his great scheme for a renewed and purified Judaism, if it had ever succeeded in reaching out to embrace great numbers of Gentiles and even Christians, some of the distinguished Christian members of this society might have played a part. Instead he had to say to them:

> So, my friends, you see before you a disillusioned, sad and embittered old man. But yet, not a hopeless old man, for he still believes in God. He refuses to bow the knee to the fashionable Zionist Baal. He refuses to succumb to Jewish nationalism, on the one hand, or to gentile anti-Semitism on the other, even though these powerful forces so powerfully react upon, and stimulate, one another. He is an extremist, a diehard, a

---

[1] Lucy Cohen, *Some Recollections of C.G. Montefiore,* London, Faber & Faber, 1940, p.225.

fanatic, if you will, but he has not lost his faith. His old ideal of the Englishman of the Jewish faith shall yet, as he believes, prevail. If it does not, then indeed, as a good Victorian, he must take refuge in the familiar saying of the Victorian poet. He must seek to believe that God fulfills himself in many ways.[2]

Although Montefiore is not recanting, and maintains his integrity as a reformer to the end, he in effect concedes defeat in the matter of his great scheme to transform the religious map of his day. For his Christian contemporaries, the conversion of Europe, America and Australia to Judaism would be unthinkable, notwithstanding any lipservice they might pay to the excellencies of the Jewish faith. To Montefiore's Jewish contemporaries, even those who supported the "Mission of Israel" concept, such a prospect would have certain nightmarish aspects. Certain rabbis such as Rabbi Alexander Schindler in America have spoken in favour of "missionary" work amongst Gentiles,"[3] as have Rabbi Roger Pavey,[4] and Rev. Leslie Hardman,[5] in England, but they have in mind more of a "replenishing the synagogue" exercise than a fully-fledged "winning the world" vision such as Montefiore cherished.

In conclusion, it should be said that a student of Montefiore's life and work does not have to agree with his aims to admire the devotion and diligence and magnanimity he showed in seeking to further them. Montefiore left this world just before the 1939-45 war which left the world a vastly different place from the one he had known. It is tempting to speculate about what his attitudes to changed conditions would have been. The great efforts of his son Leonard to help the victims of Nazi cruelty show quite clearly the philanthropic spirit of his father, and indicate the line the father would have taken. Claude Montefiore may or may not have become reconciled to the fact of the State of Israel, but certainly it could be said that his attitude to Israelis, both Ashkenazi and Sephardi, both Jew and Arab would have been benevolent and generous, as it had always been to his fellows. The inter-faith discussions between Jew and Christian which have been a feature of the post-war world would have interested him, but in the light of what was discussed in the previous chapter, it would be difficult to predict his response. Perhaps all that can be said of one with such a lively and original mind is that his response to all the challenges of our day would have been lively and original!

---

[2]ibid, pp.227-228.

[3]M.R. Wilson, "Christians & Jews: Competing for Converts?", *Christianity Today*, Carol Stream USA, March 21 1980. cf Jew. Chron. 18.12.81.

[4]R. Pavey, Jewish Information, Vol.7:1, Chicago, 1968, pp.1 & 38.

[5]L. Hardman, "Jews Should Become Missionaries," *Jewish Telegraph*, 23.10.81 (Manchester).

Selected Bibliography

The works of Claude G. Montefiore are listed in:

1. F.C. Burkitt (Ed.), *Speculum Religionis,* Oxford, Clarendon Press, 1929.
2. Lucy Cohen, *Some Recollections of Claude Goldsmid Montefiore,* London, Faber & Faber, 1940.

---

3. Israel Abrahams, *Studies in Pharisaism & The Gospels,* (2 vols.), Cambridge, Cambridge University Press, 1917 & 1924.
4. Leo Baeck, *Judaism & Christianity,* New York, Harper, 1966.
5. Steven Bayme, 'Claude Montefiore, Lily Montagu & The Origins of the Jewish Religious Union,' *Transactions of the Jewish Historical Society of England Sessions 1978-80, Vol.XXVII & Miscellanies Part XII,* London, J.H.S.E., 1982.
6. Norman Bentwich, *Claude Montefiore & His Tutor in Rabbinics,* Southampton, University of Southampton, 1966.
7. Leslie I. Edgar, *Claude Montefiore's Thought & The Present Religious Situation,* London, Liberal Jewish Synagogue, 1966.
8. Walter Jacob, *Christianity Through Jewish Eyes,* Cincinnati, Hebrew Union College Press, 1974.
9. Louis Jacobs, *Montefiore & Loewe on The Rabbis,* London, Liberal Jewish Synagogue, 1962.
10. Raphael Loewe, 'Prolegomena to Montefiore & Loewe,' *A Rabbinic Anthology,* New York, Schocken, 1974.
11. Eugene Mahaly, 'Prolegomena to C.G. Montefiore,' *Rabbinic Literature & Gospel Teachings,* New York, Ktav, 1970.
12. W.R. Matthews, *Claude Montefiore: The Man & His Thought,* Southampton, University of Southampton, 1956.
13. David Philipson, *The Reform Movement in Judaism,* New York, Macmillan, 1907.
14. W. Gunther Plaut, *The Rise of Reform Judaism,* New York, World Union for Progressive Judaism Ltd., 1963.
15. Louis I. Rabinowitz (Ed.), *Encyclopaedia Judaica,* Jerusalem, Keter, 1974.

16. John D. Rayner, *Toward Mutual Understanding*, London, Clarke, 1960.

17. S. Sandmel, *We Jews & Jesus*, Gollancz, London, 1965.

18. Solomon Schechter, *Studies in Judaism*, Vol.1, London, Black 1896.

19. Solomon Schechter, *Studies in Judaism*, Vol.2, Philadelphia, Jewish Publication Society, 1908.

20. Solomon Schechter, *Some Aspects of Rabbinic Theology*, London, Black, 1909.

21. L. Silberman, 'Prolegomenon to C.G. Montefiore,' *The Synoptic Gospels*, New York, Ktav, 1968.

22. Joshua Stein, *Claude Goldsmid Montefiore on the Ancient Rabbis*, Missoula, Scholars Press, 1977.

23. Joshua Stein, ed., *Liber Freund: The Letters of Claude Goldsmid Montefiore to Solomon Schechter, 1885-1902*, ms. to be published as part of the *Studies in Judaism* series, Washington, D.C.: University Press of America, 1988.

Index

DATE DUE

HIGHSMITH   #LO-45220